THE
SUCCESSFUL
LIBRARY TRUSTEE HANDBOOK

Mary Y. Moore

in consultation with
Association for Library Trustees and Advocates

AMERICAN LIBRARY ASSOCIATION
Chicago   2005

While extensive effort has gone into ensuring the reliability of information appearing in this book, the publisher makes no warranty, express or implied, on the accuracy or reliability of the information, and does not assume and hereby disclaims any liability to any person for any loss or damage caused by errors or omissions in this publication.

Design and composition by ALA Editions in Sabon and Benguiat using QuarkXPress 5.0 on a PC platform

Printed on 50-pound white offset, a pH-neutral stock, and bound in 10-point cover stock by McNaughton & Gunn

The paper used in this publication meets the minimum requirements of American National Standard for Information Sciences—Permanence of Paper for Printed Library Materials, ANSI Z39.48-1992. ∞

Library of Congress Cataloging-in-Publication Data
Moore, Mary Y.
    The successful library trustee handbook / Mary Y. Moore, in consultation with Association for Library Trustees and Advocates.
        p.   cm.
    Includes bibliographical references and index.
    ISBN 0-8389-0891-8
    1. Library trustees—United States—Handbooks, manuals, etc. 2. Public libraries—United States—Administration—Handbooks, manuals, etc.
    I. Association for Library Trustees and Advocates. II. Title.
    Z681.7.U5.M66 2005
    021.8′2′0973—dc22   2004017884

Printed in the United States of America

09   08   07   5   4   3   2

CONTENTS

FOREWORD

Congratulations! You've been tapped or elected to be a library board member. You are the heart of America's public libraries, that important link with the community. As a library board member you represent the community, providing insights into its needs and working closely with the library director to develop partnerships in the community.

With their myriad responsibilities, library trustees need to develop skills in advocating, policy making, planning, evaluating, hiring, budgeting, and fundraising. The Association for Library Trustees and Advocates is committed to trustee education through publications, newsletters, and continuing education opportunities. We urge you to become involved in the state and national organizations so you can network with other trustees and learn from one another, and we heartily endorse Mary Moore's book as a way to learn more about public library trusteeship.

This handbook is an excellent introduction for the novice trustee and a useful reference for the board member needing specific information on many topics impacting library boards. Whether you are elected or appointed, whether you serve on an advisory or a governing board, you will get insight into your duties and responsibilities.

Be an advocate for libraries wherever you go!

SHARON SAULMON
Past President
Association for Library Trustees and Advocates

PREFACE

Through the years, I have worked extensively with both governing boards and advisory boards, serving on some as a library director. In all my experience, the best education I ever had about boards came from one of my board chairs, John Langen in Glasgow, Montana, a prince of a guy and every library director's dream trustee. He may not have known much about libraries, but he sure understood boards and how they should operate. I leaned about boards from him and he learned about libraries from me—a perfect synergy.

Over time, I learned that John was unique in his understanding and leadership. The more board members I met in the course of my work, the more I became disturbed at the number of people who seemed to be traveling in the dark. I recently sat on a board (from which I quickly resigned) that didn't know what its responsibilities were and had a director who wasn't about to clue them in. I have dealt with boards that have micromanaged their libraries to the point of driving their directors away. I have counseled boards so unwilling to give up their turf that they have refused to join systems that would have provided far better library service to their customers. I have worked with boards that were totally unprepared to deal with budget cuts. And I have advised trustees who had inept directors about whom they could do nothing because they had never given them any performance evaluations. So many troubled boards. So much friction and anxiety. So many libraries that suffer because of people who want to do good things but don't know how. So many library trustees who are miserable because board meetings are unpleasant.

I have served on several nonprofit boards and have been surprised to discover that libraries are not alone. Furthermore, the general principles that apply to operating library boards apply to the other nonprofit boards as well. In my years of service, I have never been given a really good orientation to a board. Mentioning the need for strategic planning is usually like speaking a foreign language.

Budgets have been passed around at meetings and we were expected to give them a quick glance and say OK. I could barely get through the first line item, much less the entire budget. I have a friend who determined after she retired that she would never sit on a board again. She has had too many wretched board sessions and feels she no longer needs the grief. What a tragedy! She is the perfect board member—savvy, politically brilliant, and knowledgeable about how boards should operate.

It doesn't have to be that way. That's why I decided to help. I hope this book gives new members of both governing and advisory boards some insight and confidence. Although I wrote the book for library trustees because that's the world I know best, it should be helpful to people who sit on other nonprofit boards as well.

Because my advice can apply to any public library board situation, I have used the generic "library" throughout the book. Public libraries come in so many different governing configurations these days, and state and local laws can be so diverse, that some passages might not seem to apply directly to the reader's own situation. However, all the basic rules and principles apply to any board operating in a nonprofit environment.

I have also taught workshops in basic boardsmanship for several years. I discovered that sometimes the simple mechanics of board relationships and board meetings can foul up the operation. I hope the chapters on these two issues prove helpful. Because confusion seems to run rampant among library trustees for the first two years of their tenure, I have tried to make the basic responsibilities and how to carry them out abundantly clear. I have tried not to use jargon (another pitfall for library board members) or too many details, which can confuse rather than clarify. You won't find everything you need to know in this one book, but it is certainly a good place to start.

So I hope you enjoy this little volume. It is meant to be marked in and carried around. The questions at the end of each chapter will help you absorb what you have read, and the websites in appendix B are wonderful sources of help.

My thanks to you for your work with libraries. It is one of the most meaningful methods of public participation I can think of in this day and age.

1

Getting Started

Attending your first board meeting can be a daunting experience. You might not know anyone else on the board. You might be marginally aware of what the board does, but you might not know how the meetings will be run, how you will fit in, or what your responsibilities will be. Invariably someone will smile kindly and inform you that it will take at least two years for you to bridge the learning curve and feel productive. What a waste of time! With this book as a guide through your term on a library board, your learning curve will be shorter and less painful, and you will become productive more quickly.

Public libraries throughout the United States have boards of trustees. However, just as there is no one type of public library, so there is no one type of library board. Some of those boards are elected, some are appointed; some are advisory, some govern; some have three members, some have more than twenty. The structure and function of the board depend upon the library laws of your state and the nature of the library itself: whether it is urban, rural, small, large, multibranched, regional, municipal, county, etc. The first thing you need to do to understand your role is answer the following questions:

What type of public library do I serve as board member?

Am I a member of a governing board or an advisory board?

Whom does the library serve—what is its jurisdiction?

From where does the library receive its funding?

Board Orientation

If you can answer the foregoing questions right off the bat, you probably received a thorough orientation from the board chair and the director of the library. A really good orientation includes the following information:

- list of board members, their contact information, and their terms of office
- description of board committees
- bylaws of the board
- library's vision and mission statement and any planning documents
- copies of all current library policies
- copies of the current budget and the latest audit report
- board minutes for the last six months
- annual reports for the last five years
- diagram of organizational structure
- a copy of your state's library laws, including public meeting acts and library privacy laws
- your state's trustees manual
- description of the library's programs, services, and hours
- the most current annual statistical report and any other evaluative data
- brochures or other publications about the library

In addition to this information, you should be given a tour of the library's facilities and have a chance to talk in earnest with its director. You will want to discuss how the library is run, what relationships it has with local government and other public institutions such as schools, and what vision the director has for the future of the library. If that has not happened and you are not sure of the answers to those initial questions, stick out your neck and ask. You might even be the one who initiates a good board orientation in your library, which will definitely make you productive immediately!

The Job Description

Boards govern a variety of institutions: corporations, churches, schools, symphonies, and hospitals, to name just a few. Some boards encourage membership of people who are well known in the field; some want wealthy people who are expected to contribute to various funding campaigns; and others look for people who can represent parts of the community and act on their behalf. A library board usually consists of people in the last group.

A library board member is often referred to as a *trustee* because as such one is expected to be a good steward, or caretaker, of the library or library system. This does not refer to the physical or historical maintenance of the buildings, but to stewardship of the library's growth and success. It is also a reference to caretaking of the library needs of the community you represent. As a trustee, you are a public servant endowed with the people's trust to take care of the community's library and its citizens. If this sounds like a grave responsibility, it is. I hope you were told all of this *before* you agreed to be a member of the public library board of trustees.

There was a time long ago when library trustees were pillars of the community, appointed as a nod to their economic, political, or social status. Attendance at meetings was iffy, and the knowledge and talent required were minimal. It was not unusual for board members to excuse themselves from months of meetings because they had to go south for the winter. Things changed, however, with the advent of public library systems, changes in political and social mores, and the development of public library programs and services. Today's public library trustee needs to be politically and economically savvy, socially conscious, a quick learner, and a good team player. The truly successful trustee will also be enthusiastic about what libraries can do for the lifelong learning of the citizens they serve.

Characteristics of success

Following are common characteristics of successful board members:

- willingness to commit time and energy to the position
- desire to see the library assume an important role in the community that fully serves its customers
- record of working well with others
- willingness to make decisions

- ability to participate in discussions without taking over meetings
- knowledge of the community
- ability to advocate for the library in the community and in presentations to some units of government
- commitment to progress for the library
- willingness to consider new programs, methods, and technology to solve problems
- willingness to attend retreats, conferences, and workshops for continuing education
- willingness to participate in fund-raising

These criteria are the same for any board, regardless of the type of organization it represents. If you have been on the governing board of a hospital, YWCA/YMCA, credit union, school, fire district, or any other nonprofit organization, then you may bring valuable skills and knowledge to your new library board. One of the most important skills you can bring is the experience of acting as a body of the whole—*a group that acts in the aggregate rather than as separate individuals.* This is a difficult concept for some to grasp, but it is crucial if one is to be a successful board member.

Tasks and Responsibilities

The advisory board

What you will be doing on the library board will depend upon the type of board it is. If you are on an advisory board—one that provides counsel and recommendations to another—your position may not be very time-consuming. If you are on the board of a library that is a part of a system of libraries (library branch) or of a municipal library that is a city department, you will probably be expected to advise on the hours the library will be open, to assist in strategic planning for the library, to participate in the annual evaluation of the director, to provide policy recommendations, and to generally be an advocate for the library.

If you do become a member of an advisory board, be sure to ask what the specific responsibilities are because they may differ from one library to the next. And in some municipal libraries, the job of actually governing the library is assigned to the board through municipal ordinance.

The governing board

The responsibilities of a governing board are often more clear-cut than those of an advisory board. A governing board determines the policies of the library, sets its budget, and is responsible for hiring and firing the library director. A governing board does not answer to anyone for its decisions except, of course, to the public on whose behalf the decisions are made.

One of the most important things for a new trustee to learn is that a library board *governs* the library. It does not *manage* the library. The library director and his or her staff manage the library, with the director as the primary administrator. If there is one mistake that can sink a library and cause a capable director to leave, it is a board's misguided efforts to manage the library. Decisions regarding personnel, program development, daily operations, use of technology, collection development, marketing, financial management, program evaluation, and facility maintenance belong to the director and the staff. The board may set policies that affect these issues, but efforts to actually run the library tend to make the director feel defensive.

In a nutshell, the functions of a governing board are as follows:

- policy development
- strategic planning
- resource oversight (budget, fund-raising, liability)
- regular evaluation
- advocacy
- hiring and firing the director

Additional expectations

The aforementioned are the major functions of a board, but there are other expectations as well. Regular attendance and participation at meetings, for example, is crucial to board success. Board bylaws usually indicate the number of meetings it is acceptable to miss before dismissal, although the guidelines are rarely enforced. If you constantly have conflicts with board meeting dates and times, ask if they can be changed. However, if that just causes problems for the other board members, then it is probably best to resign.

Another expectation of a board member is that you will learn as much as you can about your responsibilities on an ongoing basis. Familiarity with a range of local and national issues that affect libraries is very important. Understanding laws governing public meetings and availability of public records; upholding the First Amendment; protecting the right to read, see, and listen; encouraging diversity; and championing literacy are all a part of a library board member's continuing education. Becoming a member of the state's library trustee association and attending workshops for trustees whenever possible can assist immeasurably with these efforts. The American Library Association sponsors a division for public library board members called the Association for Library Trustees and Advocates (ALTA). The group meets twice yearly and offers fine opportunities for learning and networking.

Finally, board members are expected to accept leadership roles. Boards usually have chairs and vice chairs who plan and run meetings, appoint work committees for special projects, and work closely with the library director in between meetings. They often represent the board in meetings with governing officials or the media.

Cheers for Volunteers

You are one of those truly blessed people known as volunteers. Surely, there is a special place somewhere in the universe for people who volunteer their time to ensure the public good. So, before we continue with our analysis of the functions of a board member, thank you!

What Have You Learned
from This Chapter?

As a rule of thumb, you absorb only about 20 percent of what you learn unless you immediately use that knowledge. Answer the following questions to reinforce what you learned in this chapter:

What type of public library do you serve as trustee?

Are you a member of a governing board or an advisory board?

From what sources does your library or library system receive its funding?

How long is your term on the board?

How thorough was your orientation to the board?

If you could change the orientation process, what would you do to improve it?

2

Relationships

Your relationships with other board members, the library director, the staff, and the community you represent are vital to your success as a trustee, yet this aspect of the job is often overlooked. The typical term for a library board member is three to five years. Reappointment usually occurs if you are willing to serve and have represented your community well. Considering the time you will be spending with all these different people, you will want to make sure that your communication lines are open and your trust levels are high—just as they should be in a good marriage.

Relationships with Other Board Members

People decide to serve on a library's board of trustees for a variety of reasons. The most laudable reason has to do with the desire to serve their community in an area to which they can bring some knowledge or talent. Unfortunately, people with personal agendas are often elected or appointed to library boards, and they can cause serious problems. Consider why the following people might be problematic:

- The person who is on the board because he or she wants to cut taxes and does not care where or how.
- The person who is on the board because he or she thinks it will look good on a political résumé.
- The person who thinks board service might be a nice social thing to do—a kind of "good works" that one can talk about at a cocktail party.

8

- The board member who is a political activist and has one issue or concern for which he or she campaigns to the exclusion of other issues.
- The board member who believes that he or she alone knows what is moral and what is immoral when it comes to the library.

You can imagine that meeting month after month with these folks might be difficult. So what can you do?

First of all, examine your reasons for being on the library board. Perhaps you had no reason other than that you were flattered to be asked. Or perhaps you started out with one thing in mind but have changed your perspective now that you know what is expected of you. A successful library board member will be open-minded, objective, and reasonable. There will be times when you have to put your own prejudices aside to do what is best for the library and the community. Always remember: a board works in the aggregate, not as individuals with opinions that are tenaciously held onto until others give up.

Another thing you can do is ask lots of questions so that you see the whole picture on any issue that is discussed. Do not be afraid of sounding ignorant or stupid. We always tell library patrons that there is no such thing as a stupid question; true ignorance occurs when someone doesn't ask, but assumes instead that others will know. You may even be doing a favor for someone who is less assertive than you. You may also prevent someone from pushing something through without telling the whole story.

Finally, if someone on your board is behaving unethically, the best thing you can do is call the person on it. It need not be done offensively. Use an "I" message such as, "I feel that when you constantly miss meetings or arrive late, perhaps you are not as committed to this responsibility as I am. Can you clarify this for me? Do we need to change the date of the meetings?" This message is very clear, but it will not offend the person because it also expresses concern for his or her welfare.

If you use these techniques, you will improve communication at your meetings and demonstrate your value as a board member.

Relationships with the Library Director

In terms of a relationship between you as a board member and the library director, there are two basic points to keep in mind.

1. It is your job to work with other board members on the *governance* of the library. It is the library director's job to *manage* the library.
2. A governing board is responsible for hiring, evaluating, and, if necessary, firing the library director. In other words, the library director is your employee. The rest of the staff are hired, evaluated, and, if necessary, fired by the director or his or her designee. With an advisory board, it is someone else's responsibility to employ the library director, although board members should be able to advise the employer on various aspects of the director's employment.

All that formality aside, the best relationship between board members and a library director is as a team working together for the good of the library and the community it serves. With any luck, you will honestly like and respect the library director for the talents and management expertise he or she brings to the job. You might even become close friends, although that could lead to difficulties. Remember that one of your responsibilities is to evaluate the library director's performance, and you must do so with objectivity and compassion. You can't let personal feelings get in the way.

Good communication is the most powerful tool you have in establishing a solid working relationship with your director. If you have questions or concerns, talking candidly with the library director is the best course of action. Most of us try to avoid conflict. We tend to talk to a third party if there is something about a person that bothers us. Somehow it seems safer—less fraught with potential conflict. However, an honest sharing of concerns or questions with your director can usually clear things up in a hurry. If what concerns you would be inappropriate to discuss with the director, the next best person to talk to would be the chair of the board.

Relationships with the Community

You are representing either a whole community or a part of one. It should be made clear at the outset that you are representing a neighborhood, an age group, an ethnicity, a business community, or perhaps a particular town or county. To that end, you need to know what your constituents want from the library or the library system. You are not expected to send out surveys or hold focus groups; that's the job of the library staff. But there are other ways to keep your finger on the pulse of your community. You can gauge the degree to which your community is being served by attending community meetings, asking questions at gatherings, and listening to what people are saying about the library.

Alice Ihrig, a library trustee from Wisconsin and past president of the American Library Trustees Association (now the Association for Library Trustees and Advocates), used to tell wonderful stories about her methods of getting feedback on her library. One of her tactics was to "accidentally" nudge the cart of the shopper ahead of her in the supermarket checkout line. When noticed, she would smile brightly, apologize, and immediately introduce herself as one of the local library's trustees. She would then ask if the shopper was a library customer and what he or she thought of the library. That approach may seem a bit daunting, particularly if you are an introvert, but it certainly worked for her.

Relationships with Library Staff

A trustee's relationship with staff of a library is probably one of the trickiest. If you are already friends with staff members, the best rule of thumb is to be discreet. Sometimes confidential matters are discussed in library board meetings, whether you are on a governing board or an advisory board. And sometimes you have to make hard budget or policy decisions that could have unfortunate effects upon your friends.

It is tempting for staff members who know a board member personally to complain about work matters or supervisors. The most common complaint is usually about the library director. Unfortunately, libraries are often managed in a hierarchical style, with several layers of personnel at different pay scales and levels of responsibility. This can cause poor morale. It is often hard for line staff to understand why librarians are paid more than they are, and at times they are resentful. When one is unhappy with one's work, the easiest person to blame is the boss.

Some of the complaints about the library director or a supervisor might be justified, but board members should not discuss these issues with staff. The wisest course of action is to review the management style and capability of the director during regular evaluation sessions. Many people in library administration received only cursory management training in library school. They need additional training and professional development on the job. This subject will be covered more thoroughly in later chapters.

Relationships with staff can be cordial and courteous. You should care about their welfare because they are the backbone of the library service. They also represent the library's greatest resource since staff salaries use 60 percent or more of an annual budget. However, you should not court close friendships with staff people while you are on the board. Discretion, tact, and diplomacy will serve you well in these relationships.

Relationships with Political Entities

The most important relationships you can have, as far as the library is concerned, are those with local, state, and federal political representatives. Government bodies at all three levels have a powerful impact on public libraries. If your library board serves a county or city, regardless of size, the county commissioners or city council members make decisions that are critical to the library's welfare. Not only do they determine the size of the county's or city's contribution to the annual library budget but they can also be instrumental in zoning decisions, bond issues, security, and other matters.

It's a good idea to attend county commission or city council meetings on a regular basis, not only to keep tabs on local matters but also to see where the community is heading in terms of its leadership. It is important to know the goals of the body that is funding the library. If its goals are not compatible with those of the library, the funding organization may not look kindly on the library. Asking questions and making comments as is appropriate within the context of the meetings, or talking to county commissioners and city council members following the meetings, will get you known as someone who cares about the county or city and its library.

How well do you know your state government representatives? Do you know who they are, and do you feel at ease picking up the phone or e-mailing them when you are concerned about an issue? If not, you need to find out how to contact them. The state government makes many decisions that affect libraries. Most states provide funding for public libraries, and state legislatures make the laws that govern the way your library operates. So you can see that the state government relationship is a pivotal one.

Finally, the federal government has been generous to libraries over the last fifty years. Not only does it supply state library agencies with federal funds, but it also gets involved in First Amendment issues, copyright issues, telecommunications costs, and other key concerns. It's great if you are on speaking terms with your members of Congress because e-mails, letters, and phone calls do make an impact on these folks.

Attending local political gatherings and meeting your representatives face to face helps your cause. Then they can put a face with a name when you contact them on behalf of libraries.

Your relationships are critical to your success as a library trustee. Make sure that they are all they can be.

What Have You Learned from This Chapter?

Answer the following questions:

Why did you decide to become a library trustee?

What kind of "I" statement could you make to a board member who continually interrupts you during meetings?

Have you taken the opportunity to sit down individually with your library director and talk about matters? If so, how did you feel about the conversation?

Do you have friends who work at the library? How will you act with them now that you are a member of the board?

Can you name your representatives in the state legislature and in Congress?

Have you ever attended a county commission or city council meeting?

3

Meetings, Meetings, Meetings

As we discussed, the decisions the library board makes will be made as a group. That means that during your term on the board, you will have many, many meetings. Undoubtedly, the bylaws you work with will be very specific as to what constitutes a quorum and by whose rules the board will operate (e.g., *Robert's Rules of Order*). What the bylaws rarely spell out are the important rules of meeting management.

How many times have you sat through meetings that were overlong, unorganized, fruitless, or confusing? How often have you thought the group was discussing one subject only to find it veering suddenly onto another? Have you attended meetings where you didn't know what would be on the agenda? Have there been times at meetings when you had no idea who was in charge? These and other annoyances take place at meetings all over the world. The reason for all this time wasting is poor meeting management, and libraries are just as apt to be guilty as any other organization.

Meeting Do's and Don'ts

Open public meetings

Most libraries have monthly board meetings. Unless your library is a private one, these meetings are mandated to be open to the public. That means they must be publicly announced—in the daily paper, on the local radio and TV stations, and certainly on the library's website—a specific number of days ahead of time. The amount of time required for notification is usually stipulated in your state's open public meeting legislation, a copy of which should be in your board notebook along with the other state and local laws pertaining to the library. If members of the community wish to attend any of the meetings, they need to be accommodated with chairs, copies of the agenda, and a time during the meeting when they may make comments or ask questions, should they choose to do so. There may even be times when the press will attend a library board meeting, and accommodation must be made for them as well.

Your role

Library board meetings are important for many reasons, but mainly because the trustees set public policy and the public must be involved in that activity. Therefore, it is essential that the meetings be run efficiently and effectively. Follow these guidelines to make sure you are doing your part to make the meetings productive:

- Always be on time and do not leave early.
- Come to the meeting prepared.
- Stay on topic.
- Do not interrupt.
- Speak up when you have something to say, but don't hog the discussion.
- Note any tasks assigned to you as a result of a board decision.
- Speak with honesty and candor.

If you do your part to help a meeting along, you will be a good model for other trustees. Certainly the board chair will appreciate you.

The meeting agenda

Those who lead the board meetings, such as the chairperson and the director, are responsible for developing the agenda. It makes sense to set the agenda—with the exception of emergency items—at the preceding meeting. That way, everyone has a chance to provide input, and items are more likely to come up in a timely fashion. Five to ten days prior to the meeting, board members should receive a copy of the finalized agenda along with any information needed for decision making. This is referred to as the *board packet*. Keep in mind that the information you receive will do you no good if you don't read it.

Setting an agenda with an eye to a meeting that runs smoothly can take some expertise. There was a time when agendas consisted of old business, new business, and reports. In the newer format, agenda items are arranged according to outcomes or expected reaction from the board members. The items are timed, and there is an indication of who will lead the discussion on each item. A typical library board agenda would look something like the following:

ST. ANNE PUBLIC LIBRARY
Board of Trustees Meeting—April 12, 2005
Agenda

Introductions and agenda review (3 min.): Newton

Approval of minutes for March 14, 2005 (5 min.): Newton

Budget report and approval of bills (15 min.): Halvorsen—ACTION

Designation of potential building sites for proposed branch library (30 min.): Newton—ACTION

Review of new laws regarding maternity leave and possible personnel policy revision (20 min.): Halvorsen—DISCUSSION ONLY

Agenda for next meeting (3 min.): Newton

Comments from the floor (15 min.): RESPONSE

Adjournment

With this type of agenda, you will know what is expected of you before the meeting. You can be well prepared and able to take part in the discussions and decision making.

Board leadership

The chairperson is usually designated to lead board meetings. The library director is expected to attend and take part in all board meetings. In some cases, the director takes the minutes of the meetings, but it is better to have an administrative assistant perform that task so that the director is free to enter discussions and provide reports. The chairperson needs to have good facilitation skills to run a successful meeting. Those skills include keeping people on track, dealing with those who interrupt or try to dominate the discussion, making sure everyone has a chance to speak, and ensuring that there is follow-through on any decisions that are made.

Executive sessions

The only meetings of a public library board that are not open to the public are executive sessions. Generally speaking, executive sessions need to be announced ahead of time following the normal meeting notification procedures, and the topic of discussion needs to be made public. However, the meeting itself is private. The reasons for an executive session usually have to do with personnel. For instance, collective bargaining sessions with employee unions, grievance or mediation proceedings, or the director's performance evaluation may be held privately according to the majority of state laws on the subject. Executive sessions may also be held to consider publicly bid contracts or real estate transactions. Always check your state's Open Public Meetings Act before proceeding with any executive sessions.

What Can Go Wrong?

Trivia

Even with the best meeting management and the most dedicated board members, things can still go wrong. The most typical error board members make is to dwell on the trivial rather than the big picture. For instance, the topic of a library fund-raiser may come up for discussion and possible action. The board might spend valuable time talking about the pros and cons of various foods to be served rather than paying attention to the desired result or the strategies for actually raising the money. When that happens, the chairperson should appoint a subcommittee to deal with the details of the project. Perhaps you feel more comfortable or more knowledgeable about the small stuff of life, but that is not the job of a library trustee.

Micromanagement

Emphasis on the trivial may waste time, but micromanagement can be even more damaging to the library and its staff. Micromanagement is defined as "controlling with excessive attention to minor details," and, sadly, it occurs in more libraries than we would like to think about. A library board of trustees exists for the purpose of governance, not management. Excessive attention to minor details may be appropriate for an accountant or a project director, but it is not appropriate in anyone who is responsible for many divergent programs or staff. The following examples of micromanagement have actually occurred in libraries across the country:

The library director provides board members with copies of the revised branch hours. The chairperson notices a change in the times of a particular branch and insists upon setting up a subcommittee to "explore" the matter.

A board member becomes concerned about the quality of the young adult books. She enters the main library in the evening, removes a professional tool from the director's office, and proceeds to check the library catalog for the top ten young adult books. Then, at the next board meeting, the trustee announces that the library only has seven of the top ten young adult books, and she wants to know why.

After reviewing the bills for a month, as is the custom in some libraries, a board member notices a purchase for pens. He notes the price per pack and takes the library director to task for not buying the pens at another store for a cheaper price.

Board members who insist on micromanaging either do not have a clear understanding of what they are supposed to be doing or they have lost trust in the management of the library. In either case, the behavior must be stopped because it is counterproductive and potentially destructive. If it involves mistrust of the library's management, that can be taken care of during the director's performance evaluation and might entail additional management training. If it is a behavioral issue, it is up to the chairperson to have a private talk with the person who has the problem.

Managing public comment

Another problem that might occur is the disruption of the meeting by people who are unhappy over something the board or the library has done or is about to do. Library trustees must deal with several contentious issues, including free speech, positioning of a library branch, and funding concerns. If a meeting cannot be conducted in an orderly fashion because of public outburst, the board may order the meeting room to be cleared and continue in session. Final action can take place only on the matters listed on the agenda, and members of the media must be allowed to remain.

Management of public comment is an important board skill. There should always be a time on the agenda for public comment, preferably at the end. Courtesy and consideration need to prevail. There will always be those who disagree with something that a public entity is doing. It is an important aspect of democracy that these folks have a chance to speak their minds. And it is important for the library board members to hear these folks so that they can keep in touch with the library's constituents.

Making Decisions

Methodology

In his book *Policy Making for Public Library Trustees* James C. Baughman says, "A good trustee identifies problems, develops solutions, and makes decisions based on his or her knowledge of specific problems in relationship to the basic principles of trusteeship."[1] That is absolutely true except for the fact that no trustee makes decisions independently of the rest of the board. The decisions are made together—in congress—and therein lies the rub.

The bylaws of your board should specify how decisions are to be made. Will you decide by majority rule or by consensus? Or perhaps you will try for consensus, and if that fails the majority opinion will hold. It is best to check out your bylaws before getting involved in any decision making. If the matter is not addressed in the bylaws, don't be afraid to ask. Your questions might lead the board to a better method for making decisions.

Many boards use a five-step process for problem solving and decision making.

1. Bring the necessary people together.
2. Define the problem.
3. Determine the most probable cause.
4. Develop possible solutions.
5. Determine the best option based on the library's strategic plan, customer desires, budget capabilities, and staff resources.

Sometimes the library director will bring up a problem for discussion and will present a number of options that he or she has already considered. In that case, your job is to decide which option is best for the library and its customers. To do so, you will have to understand the issue thoroughly and make sure the director has gone through a valid process in coming up with the options.

Follow-through

Decisions with no follow-through might as well not have been made. All too often, a group of people make a decision and then everyone expects someone else to carry it out. Hasn't that happened to you? So a decision is not fully made until the participants decide who will do what, by what time or date. If one of the steps requires you to do something, make sure you record the task and the time by which you say you can get it done. Follow-up on decisions is one of the earmarks of a really efficient and effective board.

What happens if you do not like a decision that has been made? You need to ask yourself three important questions.

1. Am I unhappy with the decision or the process?
2. If it is the process, can I try to change it?
3. If it is the decision, can I live with it?

If you can answer yes to the second or third question, you should feel better. When you make decisions as a group, sometimes the decision made will not be to your liking. If your answer to the third question is no, you may have to consider resigning from the board. However, it won't have to come to that if you can get used to the change that may have occurred.

What Have You Learned from This Chapter?

Answer the following questions:

What can you do to make sure that you participate well in meetings?

What good does facilitation do for a meeting?

Can you cite any evidence of micromanagement on your new board? Have you examples?

Is there a real process for decision making on your board?

What does your state's Open Public Meetings Act say?

Do you have a written policy regarding public input at board meetings?

NOTE

1. James C. Baughman, *Policy Making for Public Library Trustees* (Westport, Conn.: Libraries Unlimited, 1993).

4

Advocacy
A Basic Board Responsibility

Advocacy is defined as "the act of pleading for, supporting, or recommending," and as "active espousal." For a member of any board—advisory or governing, corporate or nonprofit—advocacy for the organization is an essential part of the job. Sadly, few libraries in the United States have trustees who are adept at it.

Trustees tend to leave the job of advocacy to the director, the staff, or the library Friends group. Directors and staff should advocate for their library, but their jobs entail more pressing responsibilities, such as providing services for which to advocate. Furthermore, when staff advocate for more of anything for their library, people often think they are feathering their own nest. Library Friends groups are known for raising funds through book sales, gift shops, and the like. They can be eloquent advocates for the library if they receive training and support. However, the job of advocacy is much too important to leave to those who do so many other things for their libraries. The responsibility for advocacy lies directly on library boards, and they need to start doing a uniformly better job than they have in the past.

Types of Advocacy

Lobbying

Many of us think of advocacy as asking various legislative bodies for increased funding or perhaps a change in a law to assist our libraries. As

22

important as this is, it is only one kind of advocacy, and it is called *lobbying*. There is nothing wrong with lobbying for your library, but it takes a certain amount of know-how and assertiveness to do so. If you have not done it before, get help. There are workshops and books to assist you. Lobbying is a valuable skill, and one on which democracy depends.

As a library trustee, you have great credibility with local town councils, county commissions, state legislators, and members of your congressional delegation. You were either publicly appointed or elected to your position. You are expected to have specific knowledge and experience when it comes to your library.

The first step is to become familiar with these people. Go to town council and county commission meetings and introduce yourself when it is appropriate to do so. Remember that you are also their constituent. Many states have a particular day when library supporters are urged to go to the state capital to meet with their legislators. You voted for them, and they really do want to meet you. Your congressional representatives in Washington also want to hear from you, and it is so easy these days to contact them through letters, phone calls, or e-mail.

Public relations

Another type of advocacy is public relations. Sometimes people get this term confused with publicity. Both of these activities are a type of marketing, but they are distinct from each other. Publicity is normally generated by the library staff and consists of printed materials such as bookmarks, newsletters, and posters. The website for the library is an excellent form of publicity. Public relations refers to relationships that are established between the library and other organizations that can be supportive, such as the American Association of University Women, the Chamber of Commerce, and service clubs such as Kiwanis, to name a few. Although the library director is expected to engage in public relations, library board members can do a great deal to enhance the library's image with these folks. And they, in turn, can influence their members to support the library—sometimes through fund-raising and sometimes through lobbying.

Think about other groups you belong to—perhaps the PTA, Rotary, your church or synagogue, or the YMCA. The members of these various organizations benefit from the local library and can be very effective spokespeople on its behalf.

Fund-raising as a form of advocacy

The final type of advocacy in which you should be involved is fund-raising. If your library Friends group is active, give the members lots of assis-

tance and support in their fund-raising efforts. The library can always use additional funds. If your library is involved in a capital-building plan or is trying to raise the library's levy rate, you should be on the front lines—ringing doorbells, putting up signs, speaking out on the issue, and making useful contacts. As a board member, you will need to be very publicly active.

How Is It Done?

Learn to listen

One of the major mistakes library advocates make is talking rather than listening. To advocate effectively, you must know about the issues and concerns of the people who most affect the library. Your library can be a truly wonderful place with great services. However, if those services are not important to those who pay for them, they are unlikely to continue supporting them. Under those circumstances, talking about library services is a waste of everyone's time. You need to find out what your stakeholders think is important, and that is done primarily by listening to them.

If yours is a municipal library, someone needs to attend city council meetings on a regular basis to listen to the issues the city is dealing with. By paying attention to the remarks and questions of local lawmakers, you will soon have a firm grasp of their concerns. They might be discussing zoning, economic development, literacy, or children's welfare. Only when the library can help with the concerns on the table—perhaps with the Summer Reading Program or services for those who homeschool their children—will it be wise to advocate for the library. Only then will you get the council's attention.

This same principle applies to county libraries and to library systems. Attending county commission meetings, watching televised public meetings, going to "meet the candidates" sessions, and generally keeping current with your funding authorities are the best things a true advocate can do.

Do not make the mistake of ignoring the issues, problems, and interests of your library customers. Of course, different segments of the library clientele will have different interests. The key is to find ways to keep current with the customers' needs. This will involve surveys, focus groups, interviews, and other market research tools. It is worth the time, effort, and money to make sure that your library's services are  on track with the community it serves. Only when you are well versed in the customers' needs can you advocate effectively for your library.

Ask the right questions

Many library advocates ask the wrong questions when they are trying to assess the community's needs and wants. They ask customers what the library can do for them. The question sounds innocuous and well meaning, but the suggestions it elicits might not be the sorts of things a library is set up to do. A single mother might say the library could help her out by providing inexpensive or free day care. A teenager might think it would be cool to build a roller rink outside. Someone else might suggest cooking classes. Needless to say, the library is not prepared to offer these services because they are not a part of its essential mission.

If you ask about their concerns now and down the road—about the economy, the environment, jobs, or health care—then you can consider what the library can do to help the community within the confines of its mission. Perhaps the library's book club can spend time reading about corporate development and its impact on the stock market and learning how to read the stock reports in the daily paper. Perhaps the library could feature speakers on global warming, the success rates of various recycling programs, or backyard composting with family table scraps. The video collection might be enhanced to include interview techniques and résumé-writing tips, and the library's website can include links to various job lines and to the *Occupational Outlook Handbook* online. Initiatives like these will help the library establish services its advocates can espouse with gusto.

What Do We Advocate?

A dear friend of mine was the director of a library system that received funding from both a major city and the surrounding counties. In discussing the upcoming annual budget with the city administrator, my friend was informed that the library would have to take a cut because money was tight. When she heard that the library was being asked to take a bigger cut than other city services, my friend protested, only to be told that the cut was reasonable because, after all, police and firefighters saved lives. My friend responded by asking what would be the point of saving a life if it had no quality to it—inferring that libraries provide services that enhance the quality of life.

Joey Rodger, former CEO of the Urban Libraries Council, said in a recent article that libraries must create public value. "Libraries are publicly funded because they support lifelong learning for all people. The benefits of continuous learning extend, in theory, to entire communities. If the information contained in books, videos, and the Web was available only to those who could pay for it, our communities would be poorer. . . . To sustain a stream of public funding, however, we must add value in return."[1] And so we are back to what our customers and our funding organizations think is valuable. If the community is having financial problems, you must be able to talk about how the programs and services of the library assist the community in its economic development efforts. If the community has deep concerns about the welfare of its children, you must illustrate how the children benefit from the programs at the library.

It is not enough just to say they do; you have to prove it as well by pointing to results. Are the reading scores of the children who use the library improving over those of children who do not? Are there fewer teenagers hanging about in the mall because of the new young adult after-school film program at the library? Has the jobless rate decreased because of the library's job search center? Has a new industry moved into town, citing the excellent library as an amenity for its employees?

These are the ways to advocate for your library—to illustrate its public value. It is not hard once you get the knack of speaking to the issues and concerns of others rather than those of the library. Try it and you will be amazed at how successful you can be!

What Have You Learned from This Chapter?

Answer the following questions:

What are the different types of advocacy?

Which would be better for your library or library system:

1. Going to city council meetings?
2. Going to county commissioner meetings?
3. Both?

What organizations do you belong to and how could you talk to the members about the library?

What are the names of:

1. The state legislators who represent the district in which you live?
2. The people who represent you in Congress?

Does your state library trustee association offer workshops on advocacy?

Does ALTA offer workshops on advocacy?

What value does your library bring to its community? How would you express it to your funding authority?

NOTE

1. Eleanor Jo Rodger, "Value and Vision," *American Libraries* 33, no. 1 (2002):51.

5

Policy Development

Trustees who serve on governing boards spend a good deal of their time either setting policy for the library or reviewing policies that have already been made. The library operates on a platform of policies that not only support the strategic planning of the organization but also act as guides in decision making. Advisory library boards have input in policy development and review, but they don't actually set policy. The body they advise—a city council, a county commission, or other governing body—will enact policies for the library or library system.

Policies provide the general framework for the library, specifying who it serves and how that service occurs. Policies clearly articulate the library's purposes and priorities, its relationships, and its principles. The policies of a library give the administration and staff guidance in developing procedures and activities. Every single procedure should have its basis in policy. In other words, the policies of a library are vital to its success. How well they are constructed and reviewed is up to you and your fellow board members.

Policies and the Law

There is a very important relationship between an organization's policies and the legal climate in which the organization operates. The library's policies must adhere to local, state, and federal laws. In times of stress, it is all too easy to establish a policy that takes care of a momentary problem but may be discovered to be illegal or to provoke litigation down the road. For instance, library boards across the country are dealing with the issue of computer filtering to protect children from pornography on the Internet. It would be easy enough to establish a policy stating that all library public computers will be filtered, but that would deprive adults of their First Amendment rights. And what about the rights of children to explore and learn? How much harmless but potentially valuable information is being filtered out for them?

Librarians uphold not only people's freedom to read, hear, and see what they want but also the privacy of their library records. Two current pieces of federal legislation are causing boards of trustees and school boards across the county to wrestle with statements of policy. Congress passed the Children's Internet Protection Act on December 15, 2000, and it was signed into law a week later. The act restricts the use of federal funds for public and school libraries unless these libraries follow prescribed Internet safety policies that block access to certain materials. The U.S.A. Patriot Act of 2001 broadly expands law enforcement's surveillance and investigative powers, making it possible for investigators to search and seize extant records of any patron's library use. Both pieces of legislation could be amended or repealed in the coming years. Library staff and board members will have to keep tabs on these and other new laws that impact the library in any way.[1]

How Is It Done?

The need to design a policy normally comes up in discussing a problem the library is having. Invariably someone will ask if there are any extant policies on the matter. Relevant policies are then referred to, and the board uses them to reach a decision. But sometimes the existing policy doesn't cover the problem under discussion, or there is no policy at all. In that case, the board should table the discussion for a future meeting and ask the director to draft a policy statement for its consideration.

The director will then research the issue, often investigating what other libraries have done in the same situation. He or she may work with the chair of the board to ensure that the policy statement is not only legal but reflects the desires of the general community or the particular groups of customers involved. A draft policy statement should be included in the board packet for the next meeting, and its discussion and possible passage should be an item on the next board agenda. If an issue is likely to stir public controversy, the board would be well advised to hold a public comment session before attempting to develop library policy on the matter. In any case, it is always important to consider the public ramifications of a proposed policy statement before it is formally adopted.

If the director is smart, the draft policy statement will be accompanied by a statement of procedures and possibly even a task outline. Boards often confuse a statement of policy with a statement of procedure. For instance, the schedule of bookmobile stops is a procedural matter, whereas stating that the library will provide bookmobile service on a regular basis to certain communities is a statement of policy.

Characteristics of an Effective Library Policy Statement

An effective library policy statement:

> Is in alignment with the library's mission statement.
>
> Does not conflict with the library's plans and goals.
>
> Adheres to federal, state, and local laws.
>
> Aligns with the library's other policy statements without contradictions.
>
> Treats all people with fairness and consistency.
>
> Gives clear guidance to the director and staff in implementing the policy.
>
> Protects the rights of staff and treats them with fairness and equity.
>
> Establishes overall direction without including procedural aspects.
>
> Reflects best public library practices.[2]

Types of Policy Statements

Collection policy

Basic to any library is the policy that governs the type and quality of materials it will offer to the community. Libraries today are filled with materials in many formats besides books—videos, books on tape and CD, computer software, music CDs, DVD movies, online reference resources, online magazines (called "zines") and newspapers, and a host of other reading and viewing materials. The library's collection development policy has to cover all these formats.

Intellectual freedom policy

Librarians are usually staunch defenders of the First Amendment. We are trained to understand that a library's collection must meet the needs of all—young and old, educated and not, liberal and conservative, male and female, religious and atheistic. Sometimes we joke about having materials to offend everyone. If we are truly to be considered the "people's university," the collection should have a variety of materials representing a spectrum of opinions.

There are two policy statements that every public library should adopt: the Freedom to Read statement endorsed by the Council of the American Library Association and the Library Bill of Rights adopted by ALA's governing body. These statements are regularly reframed to bring them up-to-date. You might want to make sure not only that your library has adopted these two statements but that they are in the most current form. You will find both statements in the back of this book for your reference.

You will invariably have a customer who objects to something the library has on the shelves. The usual procedure is to ask the customer to fill out a form that clarifies why the item should be withdrawn from the collection. The staff will gather all reviews of the item and give them to the director for a decision, or the director will bring the item to the board for a decision. In either case, your intellectual freedom policy will need to cover customer objections.

Personnel policy

The best resource a library has is its staff. Staff members must have clear-cut policies governing vacation, sick leave, retirement, job classification, salary schedules, performance evaluation, continuing education and training, and disciplinary action. If yours is a municipal library, the city's personnel department will already have a complete set of policies in place. If your staff members are considered city employees, then separate personnel policies are not necessary. However, if they are not a part of some other organizational staff structure, the library board is responsible for seeing that the appropriate policies are in place and that they are monitored regularly.

More and more library staffs are becoming unionized. Should that be the case in your library, there will need to be a separate policy for nonunion staff to accompany the collective bargaining agreement that the board will adopt on a regular basis. Collective bargaining agreements typically cover hours and working conditions, grievance procedures, and other personnel matters. Your state law can be most helpful in understanding what is allowable and advisable.

Customer service policy

Few libraries adopt formal customer service policies, but they should. The consistent goodwill of a library's customers is paramount to its success. The customer service policy itself should be relatively simple and positive in tone. A sample statement might read as follows:

> *Customers of the Fictional Public Library will be treated with respect, a positive attitude, and a desire to meet their needs in a timely and friendly fashion. All customers will be treated equally and fairly, regardless of age, ethnicity, or mental/physical capability.*

Customer service training for staff should be a priority. Problems can occur, particularly if the library is understaffed or is housed in a facility that is too small. In the long run, a library board that insists on good customer service and provides the resources to back it up will be rewarded.

Circulation policy

Any circulation policy needs to include eligibility criteria for borrowing; a confidentiality policy that meets the demands of the U.S.A. Patriot Act; guidelines for fines on overdue materials, loan periods, and renewals; and other policies needed for clarification of service. However, be careful that your circulation policy does not include actual procedures such as how the materials circulate. It is easy to slide into the trap of providing too much clarification. Make sure also that the circulation policy is stated in positive terms. Too many circulation policies end up being a list of what the library does *not* do rather than what it does. This gives the staff the mistaken idea that they must police the collection rather than implement its circulation.

Facilities policy

Hours of operation are often included within the facilities policy, and you need to be careful that the policy states how many hours the library or libraries will be open per week but not which hours. Hours of operation sometimes need to be changed, depending upon the season, state-mandated holidays, remodeling, or installation of technology. You should include those occasions in the policy statement. You will also want to make sure that your facilities policy covers issues such as security, meeting room use, equipment use, and the library's compliance with the Americans with Disabilities Act.

Management policy

Library boards often overlook the importance of having policies that cover obvious issues such as responsibility and authority, budgeting and fiscal control, and acquisition and ownership. However, it is always necessary to spell out who is responsible for what.

Management policies should include matters of insurance and liability. If an elderly woman slips on the library's sidewalk and breaks her hip, the library is considered liable. If the library's management fails to pay the bills of the library in a timely fashion, the library is considered liable. If a staff member is mugged in the stacks, the library is considered liable. But just who is "the library"? Well, it is a legal entity; hence the library's budget will carry the brunt of any litigation.

Because of this legal status, board members need to be covered by errors and omissions insurance to protect them from liability for making bad decisions or neglecting to act. How sad if you, as a library trustee, were forced to sell your house because the board was sued for gross negligence. More on this subject in chapter 9.

Finally, management policies should include emergency preparedness. Since the September 11 terrorist attacks, all public places must pay more attention to how to handle possible emergencies. Of course, if you live in tornado, hurricane, or earthquake country, you already know how important this is.

Internet policy

The Internet has become one of the library's most powerful information resources. Most librarians are well trained on manipulating the Internet and other computer resources for the benefit of their customers. Furthermore, most libraries have multiple computers for customer use so that people can locate their own information if they want to. These computers are available for everyone, including children.

As we have all come to realize, posting things on the Internet is fairly easy, and there are those who post unsavory and pornographic content. Filtering the content has become the primary method of ameliorating the problem and is mandated by federal law in the Children's Internet Protection Act. Protecting children from the potential dangers of the Internet while maintaining adults' First Amendment rights calls for careful policy making on the part of a board of trustees.

If your library has not yet enacted an Internet policy, or if its policy has not been reviewed lately, it behooves you to pay close attention to it. There are excellent books on the subject, such as *Developing Computer and Internet Policies for Public Libraries* published by the Bill and Melinda Gates Foundation, and countless websites where the Internet policies of other libraries are available. Following are important elements to include in a library Internet policy.

SUGGESTED CONTENT FOR AN INTERNET POLICY

Statement of the relationship between the Internet as a resource and the mission of the library

Statement of the relationship of the Internet policy to the collection development policy and other intellectual freedom policies

Statement that the library is not responsible for the content, reliability, accuracy, currency, or bias of the Internet

Statement that responsibility for guiding children in the use of all library materials, including the Internet, rests with the parents, not the library

Statement supporting the First Amendment rights of both children and adults

Explanation of the library's position on filtering, including a warning that no filtering software is 100 percent effective

Assertion that the library staff is willing to advise and assist with the use of the Internet, as it does with all other services, but will also make every effort to protect the customer's privacy and confidentiality

Statement that copyright laws are applicable to the Internet

List of prohibited behaviors and consequences (e.g., hacking, slandering, harassing, libeling other people, damaging equipment, changing equipment settings, installing other software programs)

Last Words on the Importance of Good Policies

Policy statements are a guide to decision making, but they are not written in stone. Conditions can change, laws can change, community views and needs can change. Successful trustees monitor the policies that support the library and change them when the need arises. There was a time—and there still is in some libraries—when patrons could not bring in food or drinks because of potential damage to materials. However, the other day I visited a beautiful new library that is equipped with two cold drink dispensers and a snack machine. That's quite a statement about the library system's willingness to accommodate the comforts of its customers.

Libraries tend to have too many policies, and they tend to phrase them proscriptively rather than prescriptively. It is a fine line to walk, but remember that your library's policies are public record. What would a public perusal of your library's policies say to its customers?

What Have You Learned from This Chapter?

Answer the following questions:

What is the difference between a policy and a procedure?

Have you reviewed all the library's policies?

Are there policies that you do not understand? Have you asked about them?

What types of materials does your library offer to its customers?

Does your library hold public hearings when it is considering adopting a new policy or changing an existing one?

What is your library's position on filtering for the Internet?

If a customer objects to a book or video in the library's collection, what is the review process?

Are your library's policies written in a proscriptive or a permissive fashion? Do they emphasize what's permitted or what's prohibited?

NOTES

1. See 2003 Midwinter Resolution CD20.1 in appendix A.
2. Adapted from *Washington State Library Public Library Trustee Reference Manual*, 2001.

6

Strategic Planning

One of the most important, but often overlooked, responsibilities of a library governing board is strategic planning. Advisory boards need to get involved here as well. Having a strategic plan is like having good insurance. It is always there to fall back on when there is a problem. It is also like a road map in that it tells you where the library is headed. The strategic plan should have all the answers. And it doesn't matter whether the library is a large one with many branches or a small-town library—a clearly articulated plan is still a necessity.

However, the answers will be there only if the plan is current. It is necessary not only to build the plan but also to review it on a regular basis to make sure it expresses what is presently both desirable and feasible. Annual board retreats are useful for team building as well as for reviewing the strategic plan.

Arguments against Planning

So why, you may ask, do boards often overlook this planning responsibility? What reasons do people use to avoid building a strategic plan for their library? Well, you will probably hear that it is an expensive, time-consuming, and labor-intensive undertaking. It's true that developing a strategic plan will cost money, mostly in survey and evaluation costs. And yes, like anything else that is worth doing well, it takes time and energy to develop a plan.

There are other, more disturbing, reasons why boards and administrators try to avoid planning. In many cases, they don't know how to go about the process. Many people have never done formal planning with specific steps and exact definitions. Others have been through strategic planning efforts that were exhausting, frustrating, contentious, and overly complicated. Some library directors have an allergic reaction to planning because they don't want to lose the freedom to develop programs at their own will. Boards, on the other hand, try to prevent activities that don't conform to the library's mission and goals. But the most likely reason why people don't want to participate in planning is that it requires change, and change is very hard for some folks to accept.

Why Should We Plan?

The case for why we should plan is much stronger than any of the arguments against it. Consider these benefits of a solid strategic plan:

- It clarifies the purpose of the library.
- It demonstrates accountability to funding organizations.
- It establishes priorities for spending.
- It increases efficiency of service.
- It increases responsiveness to the library's customers.
- It provides a basis for measuring the success of the library.
- It provides expectations on which to evaluate the performance of the library director.
- It identifies opportunities for the future.

In *Alice's Adventures in Wonderland* Alice asks the Cheshire Cat, "Which way should I go?" He responds, "That depends upon where you are going." When Alice admits that she doesn't know where she is going, the Cat concludes, "Then it doesn't matter which way you go!" Certainly as a good board member, you will want to know where the library is going.

First Things First

Some planning prerequisites

Before you launch into the strategic planning process, you need to lay a solid foundation for your work. That includes:

Willingness to see some things change. The changes could be moderate or definitive. If the end result is better service for library customers or better working conditions for the staff, it will be well worth it.

Competency in the strategic planning process. Trustees, administrators, and staff should all have a basic understanding of the strategic planning process. If training is needed, look to your state library consultants for assistance. Publications such as Sandra Nelson's book *The New Planning for Results: A Streamlined Approach* (ALA, 2001) can also serve as good resources.

Funds and staff time allocated for planning. The amount depends upon the size of the population that is served by your library or library system. It also depends upon what type of public library you serve. If you are on the board of a municipal library, the city may include the library in an annual survey of service and thus save the library from having to do this on its own.

As a veteran of many planning processes, I urge you to consider finding a facilitator once you have met the foregoing prerequisites. Good facilitators help a thinking process to run smoothly and can save the library a great deal of time. They also provide insight into various methods of brainstorming and decision making. You may have to pay for a facilitator's time, but it is worth every penny. Your state library may be able to help you find a facilitator for your purposes.

Who should be involved?

Believe it or not, this is a hard question to answer. As a rule of thumb, the more people who are involved in the planning process, the more likely it is that the plan will succeed. On the other hand, large numbers of people on the planning committee can be hazardous. The ideal size for a group of planners is between seven and nine, although a group of between nine and eleven might also work. The group should consist of two or three trustees, the library director, two or three staff representing all levels of work, a representative of the governmental entity to which the library or library system answers, and one or two good library customers. To include other stakeholders in the process, it would be wise to convene various task forces that will concentrate on specific tasks.

Trustees often ask why it is necessary to involve staff in the planning process. The answer is clear. Staff members have a great stake in the future of the library. It is, after all, their working future. Staff also possess a great deal of knowledge about how the library operates—sometimes more than the director. Staff acceptance of the new strategic plan is critical, and if they feel that they have been integral to the process of building it, they will find wonderful ways to implement the plan.

Roles of board, staff, and administration

Table 6.1 shows how to delegate planning responsibilities among the board, staff, and director.

What do you need to know?

Perhaps the most important prerequisite to the planning process is known in planning parlance as the *environmental scan*. What it means is that you need to have facts and stakeholder opinions about the library and the

Board members	Director	Staff
Initiate the process	Guides the process	Understand and support the process
Ensure the quality of the process	Educates and motivates staff	Base work plans on strategic directions
Participate in the process	Sees that critical success factors are in place	Make daily decisions based on established goals
Review and evaluate the outcome	Has ultimate responsibility for implementation	Measure the success of the plan

TABLE 6.1   Areas of responsibility in the planning process

community from customers, parents, educators, city or county officials, and businesspeople. You can gather this information through surveys, focus groups, and interviews. Much can also be determined from recent statistical and demographic data, usually available from city and county websites.

Another part of the environmental scan is an interesting exercise in which the planning group brainstorms the following:

Internal strengths. What particular strengths of the library can assist in making the future positive—e.g., highly capable staff, good management, excellent collection.

Internal weaknesses. What sorts of things might weaken the library's chance of a successful future—e.g., old facilities, adversarial relationships within and outside the library, outmoded technology, staff recruitment problems, insufficient parking.

External opportunities. What is happening in the community, state, and nation that bodes well for the library—e.g., consistent healthy funding from the library's funding authorities, availability of federal grants, good political relationships, a growing population.

External threats. What is happening in the community, state, and nation that might threaten the library's future—e.g., economic downturn, dwindling local population, pressure on First Amendment issues, decreased assistance from the state library.

The results of your fact finding will add immeasurably to the planning process. Planning within a vacuum is a dismal waste of time and can make us look like we don't know what we are doing.

Steps in the Planning Process

The mission statement

A well-crafted mission statement is one of the library's most precious assets. It is a succinct statement of the library's purpose or reason for being. It should describe the *function* the library performs, *for whom* the library performs it, and *why* it is valuable to the community. It should be brief or no one will pay any attention to it. If it can be expressed in one sentence, all the better.

A quick survey of the websites for various public libraries across the nation turned up the following examples of good mission statements:

> The mission of the XYZ Community Library is to provide the highest quality library service to our citizens for lifelong learning, cultural enrichment, and enjoyment.

> The XYZ Public Library, through its collections, staff, and resources, provides residents free and equitable access to information needed for full participation in the community and for the enrichment of individual lives.

> It is the mission of XYZ Local Library to assist members of the community in educating themselves and enhancing their personal, business, and social well-being through the use of library resources and services.

> It is the mission of XYZ City Library to ensure the preservation and transmission of society's knowledge, history, and culture, and to provide the people of XYZ City with free and open access to information for education, recreation, and reference.

> The mission of the XYZ Village Library is to be a community doorway to reading, resources, and lifelong learning, and a center for people, ideas, and culture.

The mission statements of these various libraries make it clear not only what the libraries do, for whom, and why the work is important but also what they think their communities care about. The libraries that developed these mission statements are from all over the nation. Unfortunately, most of them are larger libraries; the search turned up few mission statements from small public libraries. The search also illustrated the difficulty of finding the statements on library websites. One usually needs to go about three layers down into the website to discover anything about the library and its planning. Good mission statements deserve to be on the front page.

The vision statement

While the mission statement is used to describe what *is*, the vision statement is used to express what *could be*. Generally speaking, the vision comes from the director—from his or her passion for providing the best library service possible. Vision statements do not have to express what currently exists, but they do have to be attainable. "A library on every block" may sound good as a vision statement, but it certainly isn't realistic. Here are some very good vision statements that are currently being used:

> The Ideal Public Library will be the primary gateway to a universe of information to meet the lifelong needs of the citizens of our community.
>
> We will be an example of excellence in providing library services to a diverse community.
>
> The XYZ Public Library—offering opportunities to seek, find, know, and imagine.

It is smart to make sure that your library's vision doesn't conflict with the community or area the library serves. Or, put another way, be aware of the vision statements for your city, town, or county and try to help the vision statements complement one another. It is good politics and good sense. For instance, if your town's leadership is particularly concerned with offering opportunities for children, it would behoove the library to emphasize that aspect of the service and express it in the vision statement.

The goals

Goals are statements of results that need to occur to help the library accomplish its mission or achieve its vision. Goals or results can also be considered strategies—ways to get you where you want to go. When planning, it is wise not to include more goals than it is feasible to manage within a year or two. Staff and administration need to feel a sense of accomplishment. It is recommended that the library planners choose no more than five or six goals to work on at any one time.

Following are examples of goal statements:

The ethnic diversity of the community will be reflected in the library's collection, services, programs, and staff.

Each branch library will have sufficient numbers of computers to satisfy the needs of the customers.

Library facilities will be attractive, structurally sound, handicapped-accessible, and secure.

Library collection and staff will be considered critical to the success of homeschoolers in the community.

The timeline, the tasks, and the measurements

It is appropriate for the strategic plan to include a timeline for the achievement of the goals, but it should be developed in conjunction with staff and administration. The board then needs to hold them both accountable for attaining those goals within the agreed-upon time.

The critical question then becomes "How do we know at what point the goal is accomplished?" This is when the staff and administration really get to work. They will need to list the tasks it will take to accomplish the goal, who has lead responsibility, how long each task will take, and what it will cost. From that information, they will be able to give the board specific criteria by which to measure the achievement of the goal.

If the goal were to be to have the community's ethnic diversity reflected in the library's collection, programs, services, and staff, certain tasks would be required. For instance, if the ethnic group being focused on were Hispanic, the following tasks would serve to illustrate the achievement of that goal:

Hiring four Spanish-speaking staff for the circulation desk.

Expanding the collection to include 30 percent Spanish language and music materials.

Starting a yearlong program in Hispanic literature.

Planning celebrations for Cinco de Mayo and other Hispanic holidays in the children's department.

The Celebration

Although planning is an ongoing process for the board and staff of the library or library system, it is important to celebrate achievements along the way. Staff members may celebrate by themselves, but it is very special when the board recognizes staff efforts. The recognition can take many forms—a party, a congratulatory note, a newspaper article, a commendatory report to the city or county council, or even a delivery of flowers for the circulation desk. Any effort on the board's part will certainly be appreciated.

Members of the board also need to celebrate their part in all these efforts. There is nothing wrong with having a board meeting followed by a party!

What Have You Learned from This Chapter?

Answer the following questions:

What are three benefits of strategic planning?

How ready do you think your board and your library are to change the way they do things?

What is an environmental scan?

Can you find a mission statement for another organization in your town? Do you think it is a good one?

Just for practice, what are three goals for yourself for the coming year?

If your library or library system already does strategic planning, how often does the director report on its progress? Do you feel you are sufficiently informed?

If your library already has a strategic plan, is it used in decision making at board meetings? If not, what can you do about it?

7

Evaluate, Evaluate, Evaluate

A board of trustees that doesn't evaluate library programs, customer service, the director, or itself is like an ostrich with its head in the sand. Sooner or later, someone is going to come along and pull its tail feathers out.

Evaluation is really a matter of getting continuous feedback and making adjustments when necessary. As a trustee, you should want to know that you are being accountable to the citizenry. You should want to know that you are spending the public's money wisely on their behalf. You should want to know that the library's programs and services are effective, make a positive impact on the community, and are of public value. You should want to know that you are making progress toward the goals you helped to develop in the strategic plan. You should want to know that you have a competent and talented director at the helm of your organization. And finally, you should want to know that you and your colleagues on the board are doing the best job you can.

The question, then, is how to evaluate the library's programs and policies effectively. And who should be conducting the evaluation? At this point, you are probably saying, "But I am only a volunteer!" That's true, but you are a volunteer in one of the most important jobs in your community, and there are ways to do your job successfully without going AWOL from your family. Let's take a close look at the whole evaluation responsibility and break it down into doable tasks.

Evaluating Library Programs

What is a library program?

Libraries do many things—sometimes too many—and different libraries sometimes do different things. However, there are some basic programs for which all public libraries are known:

- circulation of materials
- reference services
- children's programs
- young adult programs
- interlibrary loan
- outreach services to the homebound and to the incarcerated

Some libraries also offer programs such as:

- bookmobile or rural delivery of materials
- genealogy research
- book discussions
- readers' advisory
- computer training
- information literacy training

As you can see, there are lots of potential library programs to evaluate.

Why is program evaluation important?

In her "Basic Guide to Program Evaluation" Carter McNamara maintains that too many program evaluations generate information that is irrelevant and unusable. She feels that the "20-80 rule" should apply to program evaluation, where 20 percent of the effort generates 80 percent of the needed results. The effort should focus on utility, relevance, and practicality. Instead of getting involved in what many people think is a highly complex and unique process, board members just have to commit to understanding what is really going on. The author notes that "many people regularly undertake some nature of program evaluation—they just don't do it in a formal fashion so they don't get the most out of their efforts or they make conclusions that are inaccurate. . . . Consequently, they miss precious opportunities to make more of a difference for their customers and clients, or to get a bigger bang for their buck."[1]

McNamara goes on to discuss why program evaluation is helpful. "Program evaluation," she says, "can [help to] understand, verify or increase the impact of products or services on customers or clients. These 'outcomes' evaluations are increasingly required by nonprofit funders as verification that the nonprofits are indeed helping their constituents. Too often, service providers (for profit or nonprofit) rely on their own instincts and passions to conclude what their customers or clients really need and whether the products or services are providing what is needed. Over time, these organizations find themselves in a lot of guessing about what would be a good product or service, and trial and error about how new products or services could be delivered."[2]

There are three other reasons why program evaluation is important to a library board. First, evaluation of the programs can help you determine whether your library has met its goals or not. Evaluation can also be used for public relations and for promoting services. Finally, it is imperative to have the library's programs evaluated on a regular basis because there will come a time when the library's budget is cut. At that time, you will have to know which programs are the least effective and therefore the most likely to be cut.

What must you do about program evaluation?

The most important thing for you as a trustee to do in program evaluation is to decide what you need to know to make a decision. What do you need to decide as a result of the evaluation? What kinds of information do you need? From what sources should the information be collected? Who needs to hear from you regarding the evaluation and your decisions?

The various kinds of information that can be mined in an evaluative process are:

> *inputs*—what is needed to run the program (e.g., funds, facilities, staff, materials)
>
> *processes*—how the program is carried out

outputs—units of service (e.g., number of customers using the service, number of books circulated, number of questions answered)

outcomes—impacts on the customers (e.g., higher degree of literacy)

Given this background information, you simply need to ask your director and staff to find the answers to your questions. You will not be expected to actually cull numbers, interview clients, observe processes, or do the work that is required. You may, however, need to allocate funds for the evaluation. This funding can be used to hire outside, objective assistance or temporary staff to fill in for those who will actually do the evaluation.

To wrap up this discussion, you need to understand the importance of program evaluation. A good starting point is to list the things you need to know in order to make decisions. Program evaluation should not be done in a pinch if you can help it. If programs are evaluated on a regular basis, you and your board colleagues will be ready to make decisions about potential budget cuts (or unexpected increases) and ongoing customer complaints. Evaluation enables you to verify that you are doing what you think you are doing and makes your job of advocating for the library much easier.

Evaluating Customer Service

Why is customer service so important?

When I moved to the town in which I currently live, I had to use the local public library as a customer for the first time in my life. In the past, I had either been the director of the public library or had served in an administrative capacity. I had immediate access to any recreational reading or research material I needed without leaving work.

It took only one visit to my library branch to convince me that I would be better off going somewhere else. It had nothing to do with the location of the facility—it was within walking distance of my home. It had nothing to do with the hours—it was open nearly 60 hours a week. And it had nothing to do with its collection—it was a five-county library district with a huge collection and an excellent delivery system. It had to do with the fact that no one looked me in the eye, no one smiled at me, and no one seemed to care whether I found what I needed or not. Customer service in that library was nonexistent.

Unfortunately, although that situation has changed radically in my local library, it remains the case in many other libraries all over the nation. When public libraries were started in the United States by ladies' clubs, there was a feeling that only the genteel should be allowed to check out books. One was a "patron" of the library (and still is). The public library then became a middle-class institution serving those who were "deserving." We had images of "Marian the Librarian," a gray-haired woman in bifocals frowning and admonishing one to "Shhhhhhh." Service meant having plenty of books on the shelves—and heaven help you if you put one back in the wrong place!

This attitude stems largely from the fact that early on, the library had no competition. It was the only game in town unless you were rich enough to buy your own books. Nowadays, there is plenty of competition. Megabookstores like Barnes & Noble and B. Dalton have cropped up in malls all over the country, and they have great customer service to boot. Then there are the paperback exchanges that can be found in almost every small community. But the really big competitive force is the Internet. Answers to questions can be found on the Internet; maps can be printed off the Internet; magazines can be read on the Internet; videos and any kind of music you could possibly want are available on the Internet; and many books are being digitized for availability just as fast as people can process them. Libraries have become a choice rather than a unique service.

What do most people expect in terms of service?

Much marketing research has been done on public expectation of service regardless of where that service is offered. Customer service is not something most of us think about, but we certainly know it when we get it and we can be very annoyed when we don't get it.

The marketing research tells us that we expect the following basics in terms of good service:

- immediate eye contact or acknowledgment of our existence
- a smile
- offers of assistance
- competent employees
- efficiency

Even in these days of competitive services and shrinking local tax dollars, staff people in public libraries still make the mistakes of putting routine duties before customers, being unaware when someone needs assistance, making rules more important than customers' needs, concentrating on the troublesome few rather than the pleasant majority, and staring at a book or a computer monitor, giving the impression that they are too busy to answer customers' questions. As more and more public libraries install automated self-checkout and check-in stations, there is even less human contact. Customers begin to feel like  a library card number—faceless and inhuman. Libraries could become more and more like Automats—and you don't see those around anymore.

Negative effects of poor customer service

Poor customer service can produce unwanted results. Use will decrease; people will complain; teens may become rowdy and abusive; fewer and fewer children will be allowed to come to the library; and there may be concerned letters to the editor of the local paper. When it comes time for annual funding, city councils, county commissioners, and other funding bodies may be reluctant to provide any additional dollars. In fact, feeling that the library is not doing its job, they may very well cut the funding. But the worst result of poor library service will be an inability to pass any sort of bond issue, raise the taxation level for district libraries, or be successful in any kind of capital-building campaign. No one is likely to vote in favor of funding a service that is considered poor.

What needs to be done?

Evaluating customer service satisfaction is just as necessary as evaluating the programs the library offers. However, it is impossible for library staff to do this and there are much better ways of obtaining the information. You could hire a marketing consultant to do a huge survey, but that would be an expensive undertaking, and it might not be worth it unless you as a board feel that there are serious problems. At the other end of the spectrum, you could ask a group of your friends about their experiences with the library. The drawbacks to this method are a lack of objectivity (respondents knowing that you are on the board) and probably a lack of diversity in age, income level, and ethnicity. One of the best methods would be to hire a marketing firm to perform a "secret shopper" evaluation. The firm would hire a group of people representing the library's diverse constituency who would use the library and report back on specific aspects of customer service—creating a "report card" of sorts.

What can you and the other members of the board do if you receive a negative report? You will begin by asking your director to take action to improve the situation within a certain amount of time. You may authorize funding for training, intervention, or incentives such as Customer Service Employee of the Month. The most important thing to remember is that you don't want your library to go the way of the Automat!

Evaluating the Director

As a trustee of a governing board, you are responsible for hiring and, if necessary, firing the library director. The library director is an employee of the board. There are cases in which, as a member of an advisory board, the library director is an employee of the city, but you may have a good deal to say about his or her employment nonetheless. There are also cases where the library director may be considered an employee of the funding authority, but the board has governing powers. No matter what the employment structure is, you will be asked to evaluate the library director's performance.

Why is this evaluation so important?

There are good reasons for evaluating your library director on a regular basis. Periodic evaluation:

> Establishes a line of communication between the director and the board.
>
> Ensures that the goals and strategies of the strategic plan are being met.
>
> Identifies concerns of the board or the director.

Demonstrates sound leadership, accountability, and governance on the part of the board.

Provides a sound basis for merit raises or corrective action.

How is this done?

Good evaluation methodology can consist of both subjective and objective measures. However, keep these three caveats in mind:

1. The purpose of any performance evaluation is to encourage strengths and discuss areas for improvement.
2. There should be no surprises in a formal performance evaluation.
3. The person being evaluated should understand the basis of the evaluation.

The first step is to sit down with the other board members and the library director and determine the criteria on which the evaluation will be based, the format, and the process by which it is to be carried out. If you are a member of an advisory board and the library director is an employee of a city or county, the evaluation method will probably already be in place. It will be developed by the human resources department of whoever formally employs the director. You, as an advisory board member, may be asked to provide input. If this is not happening, you and other members of the board should ask to be included.

There are three types of criteria used for performance evaluations: library goals, the job description, and behavioral traits. I recommend using all three as long as there is a rating system on which to base an objective score. And if a low rating is given, suggestions for improvement must be provided. Board members need to agree upon the definitions of the ratings so that they are all on the same page.

Using library goals as a factor

Library goals are probably the easiest yardstick to use in evaluating the director. The question could be: Are the goals as set forth in the strategic plan being met according to the timeline stipulated for them? (1—no progress; 2—some progress; 3—timeline being met in majority of goals; 4—timeline being met in all goals; 5—all goals achieved) Or the goals can be taken individually and achievement can be rated on each one.

To determine the ongoing achievement of goals, board members should be receiving regular monthly reports from the director. Those reports need to include the progress made on the goals set forth in the current strategic plan.

Using the job description as a factor

There are some constants in job descriptions for library directors. They are such things as "prepares and manages the budget in a professional manner," "is aware of current library practices," "maintains good relationships with funding authorities," "is familiar with and utilizes technology wisely," "works closely with the board of trustees in pursuing a successful library program," "illustrates sound staff development practices," etc. All of these aspects of the library director's job description can be used as criteria in a performance evaluation. You hired the library director based on these performance expectations and you have every right to be assured that they are being carried out.

Following are specific criteria that could be included in a performance evaluation based on the director's job description:

- Monthly budget reports are completed in a timely manner.
- Innovative library practices are considered on a regular basis.
- The collection is up to date and well used.
- Relationships between staff and management are positive.
- Library director meets regularly with members of the funding authority.
- Staff development is pursued vigorously.
- Board decisions are implemented in a timely fashion.

These statements would then be rated and recommendations for improvement would be made.

Using behavioral characteristics as a factor

Using behavioral characteristics as a factor in a performance evaluation can be tricky but also very helpful. The normal behavioral characteristics considered would be such things as decision-making ability, communication skills, cooperation, dependability, creativity, leadership skills, risk taking, initiative, listening skills, etc. Sometimes these traits are listed in the job description and sometimes they are just expectations of the board. However, if the board members have not communicated these expectations to the director, they can't be included in a performance evaluation. Be very careful when including subjective factors in your evaluation; when you do include them, make sure the traits are being evaluated on the basis of firsthand observation.

Who performs the evaluation and who has input?

The people taking part in the formal evaluation process differ from library to library. Advisory board members may have input, but only sometimes do they get to take part in the performance appraisal interview. The interview is usually handled by the director of the human resources department in these cases. Some governing boards may decide that everyone wants to be part of the process. Others may decide that only the chair of the board and one other member will perform the evaluation with input from the entire board. Whatever the process, it is important that the situation be businesslike but not intimidating. Performance evaluations should be an ongoing part of a person's job, with the intent of helping that person to develop.

Board members are not the only ones who should have a chance to voice their opinions on the library director's performance. The director is also accountable to staff members, elected officials, people he or she works with in the city or county, members of the general public, Friends of the Library, and others. Input from a representative sample of those folks is very helpful, bearing in mind that the process of getting their opinions must be the same as that for gathering board members' input. It may seem easier just to ask someone what he thinks of the director, but the answer to an open-ended inquiry may have nothing to do with the director's performance. The fairest approach is to ask these people to respond to the evaluative instrument you have developed.

The performance appraisal interview

Once the board chair receives all the input, you are ready to write up the formal evaluation. Allow enough space in the written document for notes on improvements that need to be made and deadlines for completion. Distribute copies of the evaluation to the library director and all board members.

The evaluation interview should take place at a regularly scheduled board meeting. Since personnel matters are not usually discussed in open sessions, you will need to conduct the interview in an executive session before or after the business meeting. Don't forget to check your Open

Public Meetings Act to make sure you are performing the interview within the laws of your state.

When going through the evaluation, try to provide specific examples wherever possible to clarify your expectations of the director. Encourage free discussion so that all the issues can be explored thoroughly. Honesty and candor should be the rules of the interview, and there should be no interruptions. When improvement is called for, ask the library director what he or she expects to do about the problem and when it will be corrected. Include that information in the written notes of the interview. The library director should then be held to account by the board. This is referred to as *corrective action*. It is also important to provide praise and support when it is merited.

This is not an easy process, but evaluating the library director is one of the most important things that you can do for the success of the library and for the director's professional development.

Evaluating Yourselves

You probably thought you were through with all the evaluating you have to do. But is it fair not to evaluate yourselves? Aren't you interested in seeing how well you are doing as a board? You may be a wonderful trustee in a group with other wonderful trustees, but how well do you do together? Finding out isn't all that hard. It's what you do about it that counts.

How is it done?

There are two main ways to evaluate the board. You can hire someone from the outside to do it, or you can do it yourself. Most board members who are smart enough to evaluate themselves at all think it is easier and less expensive to self-evaluate. But there are pitfalls in this method that you need to be aware of before using just any board self-evaluation checklist.

There are all kinds of nonprofit boards that share many of the same responsibilities, visions, and goals. And, of course, there are many library boards throughout the nation. But each board is unique, and so the evaluation form should be unique in its identification of you. If your board already has a self-evaluation tool, it should be available in your orientation packet so that you know what is expected of you up front. If it is not available, everyone on the board needs to know what will be included in the tool so that all are prepared when the time comes to perform the self-evaluation.

I have never known a board of trustees that had the time to assess everything it does, so don't worry about being comprehensive. The important thing is to arrive at a good sense of your combined strengths and areas that need improvement. A really good time to perform a self-evaluation is at your annual board retreat, where you have the time and the relaxed atmosphere to be reflective.

Sample questions

The United Way of King County, Washington, has a board self-evaluation format that could be useful as a template. Board members react to the following statements on a scale of 1–5, with 1 being Very Unsatisfied and 5 being Very Satisfied.

How satisfied are you that the board:	Very Unsatisfied				Very Satisfied

1. Understands and can convey the organization's mission and purpose?   1   2   3   4   5
2. Knows whether or not the organization is in compliance with federal, state, and local regulations?   1   2   3   4   5
3. Knows enough about the organization's programs and services?   1   2   3   4   5
4. Provides financial oversight for the organization, including approving a realistic budget?   1   2   3   4   5
5. Appreciates the respective roles of the board, staff, and director?   1   2   3   4   5
6. Contains an appropriate range of expertise and diversity to make it an effective governing body?   1   2   3   4   5

Follow-up

Once the areas of improvement have shown up in the ratings, it is important to follow up with a commitment to using what you have learned. You might decide to institute a training program for yourselves or to attend trustee workshops that your state library makes available. You might become determined to recruit differently the next time your board has a vacancy, or you might ask your director for a special review session on certain subjects. You might even review your board orientation to make sure it is complete. Whatever you do, it will be a step forward in helping you to be successful.

What Have You Learned from This Chapter?

Answer the following questions:

What are the four areas of evaluation that a trustee must address?

Does your board currently evaluate the library's programs? If so, how?

Is your library making progress toward its current goals?

How do you know if your library's customer service is really good?

Have you asked people lately what they think of the library? If so, how did you do it?

Do you have an evaluation process set up for the library director? If so, how does it work?

Have you seen the library director's job description?

Does your library board evaluate itself? How often?

Does your board have an annual retreat?

NOTES

1. Carter McNamara, "Basic Guide to Program Evaluation." www.mapnp.org/library/evaluatn/fnl_eval.htm.
2. Ibid.

8

Hiring and Firing a Director

A capable library director is the greatest perk a board of trustees can have. A person who knows the job, communicates well, has a good sense of humor, and appreciates the efforts of volunteers is a joy to work with. That's why choosing a director is one of the most important decisions a board can make. The recruitment and hiring process will likely take several months, but the more diligent you are, the greater your satisfaction will be when the effort results in a really good director.

The Board's Role in the Process

The role the board takes in the hiring process depends upon the size and type of public library and on whether the board is a governing or an advisory body. As an advisory board member, you may have the opportunity to participate in the process, but you will not design it. Others will do that in line with their own hiring practices. Large libraries or library systems will have a human resources department that will work closely with you in designing and implementing the hiring process. If you are on the board of a small library, regardless of its funding authority, you will be on your own. In either case, if you have the funds to do it, you can hire a consulting firm to handle the process for you until it is time to interview and select the candidates. No matter what your role is, you should be familiar with the overall hiring process.

Defining Your Steps

Step 1
Determine the library's future needs and develop a profile of your ideal candidate

Reread your personnel policies and procedures to make sure you understand the hiring process. Find out, for instance, whether the library pays for a job candidate's travel and expenses. (Candidates interviewing for the director's position should be funded.) You might have to make budget adjustments to cover travel, job advertisements, and other expenses of the search.

Once you have a handle on the hiring process, you need to engage in a good old-fashioned brainstorming session with your board colleagues to determine the future needs of the library. Examine the library's strengths and weaknesses. Look at what is happening in the community that will affect the library in the coming years. (If you have recently completed your strategic plan, this information will already have been determined.) Also think about how the new director needs to divide his or her efforts between internal management and external community relationships.

Generally speaking, the director of an independent public library (one that isn't allied with a library system) that serves more than 5,000 people should have an ALA-accredited master's degree in library science (MLS) plus at least five years of experience. The larger the library, the more experience the director will need. Check with your state library or your state law to see if there are mandated minimum qualifications.

After the brainstorming, begin to list the knowledge, skills, and abilities you think will be needed to deal with the issues you identified. It is tempting to take a generic list of stereotypical characteristics and plug them in, but that would be doing a disservice to your library. Your list of attributes needs to be relevant to your library's circumstances. For instance, if the library doesn't enjoy a good relationship with its funding authority, you will want to look for someone with a track record of dealing well in the political arena. Perhaps employee morale might be low, in which case you will want someone with proven abilities in staff development and management. If there is a new library building campaign on the horizon, you will be looking for someone who has experience in that area or excellent public speaking abilities. It would be helpful at this point to ask staff, customers, and other stakeholders what they think the new director's strengths should be.

"One attribute that always seems to be necessary to perform effectively as a nonprofit director but frequently seems to be overlooked is the ability to maintain personal and professional equilibrium in the face of overwhelming demands on limited resources. . . . The inability to temper a passionate dedication to the agency's purpose and objectives with a realistic acceptance of the limits imposed by available resources frequently contributes to dysfunction in the management of nonprofit agencies."[1]

Most librarians are passionate about libraries and the programs associated with them, but few of them receive thorough management training while attaining their degree. Those interested in becoming library directors need to have pursued additional study in the area of management to handle the job well. Many librarians interested in administration attain not only the MLS but also a master's degree in public administration (MPA). Therefore, it would be wise to add to the list of qualifications either evidence of management training or a solid track record of management expertise.

Before completing the candidate profile, the board will have to agree on a salary range. It would be wise to get outside assistance in matching the list of desired attributes with a commensurate salary. If the funds aren't there, it may be necessary to limit the knowledge, skills, and abilities required. Some advertisements for library directors list so many attributes that the successful candidate would have to be able to walk on water. Then they offer a salary that would be suited to a bank clerk or a garbage collector!

A good deal is riding on this profile. If it is well written, you can use it to develop a clear and concise job advertisement, objective criteria for screening applicants, interview questions, and a framework for evaluating the finalists.

Step 2
Plan a hiring strategy and recruit job applicants

Before going any further, you and your board colleagues need to outline the rest of the tasks in the hiring process, indicate who is responsible for getting them done, and develop a timeline for completion. This will give you a good sense of your time commitment and the amount of assistance you will need. The staff will also get a sense of when they will be likely to get a new director. Change is always stressful. The more the board can keep communication open with the staff regarding the process, the less anxious the staff will be.

Your next task is to provide for an interim director. The perfect solution would be to keep the departing director in place until you hire a new one, but that is a rare occurrence, and you certainly do not want to retain someone you have had to fire. If there is a good assistant director, he or she is the obvious choice (unless that person will be a candidate for the position). Other members of the staff might also fill the bill. You could hire an interim director from outside the staff, or you could ask a retired library director to come back into harness for a few months, provided the person has the requisite abilities and you have the funds to pay him or her.

With your hiring strategies in place, you are ready to appoint a search committee. If you want to involve others beyond the board, the search committee can include representation from the staff, clientele, Friends of the Library, the city council or county commission, the local school board, and other stakeholder groups. Some members of the board may opt to work on the search committee and some may not. The search committee can review the applications, cull through the candidates, and narrow the field down to those the entire board will want to interview.

Now you are ready to advertise for the position. Large city newspapers can be useful, particularly if they are from within your state. Professional journals such as *American Libraries* and *LJ Hotline* can also work, but they will need some lead time before they publish your ad. Other outlets are the various websites that carry advertisements for library jobs such as www.ala.org, www.lisjobs.com, or, in the Pacific Northwest, www.pnla.org. State libraries list jobs on their own websites, and you might also check your state library association's website. Word of mouth always works well in the library profession, so be sure to share your job announcement with the staff. And, of course, the job description and application should be available on your own library's website.

Step 3
Screen applicants

Applications from job candidates will probably take from two to six weeks to come in, so you will need to set your deadline accordingly. Since the applications have to be kept confidential, one person should receive them. If you do not have a human resources department, perhaps you could entrust one of the staff or the board chair to screen the applications. All members of the board should receive copies of the ones that qualify. Remember that the application process gives you only the basics and some inferences regarding the candidates' suitability.

After the deadline, review the applications together as a board and determine which candidates you want to interview. Most boards or search committees invite three to seven candidates to interview for a job. Some of these applicants may be internal, and they should be considered equally with those from outside. It is customary for the invitation to interview to be extended in writing and accompanied by information about the library and the community it serves. The library's budget, the strategic plan, advertising brochures, and materials distributed by the chamber of commerce would be helpful to applicants.

Step 4
Assess applicants

At this point, you and the other board members need to design the interview process. The interview itself should be based on the job description, with questions that will help you determine if the candidate can fulfill the job requisites. Most interviews should last no more than an hour to an hour and a half. Make sure you have a system for rating the candidates' answers to each question and that all members of the board have the same understanding of the ratings, such as what will constitute high, medium, or low rankings.

Remember that job candidates can tell the interviewers what they want to hear without having to back it up. That's why it's a good idea to observe their behavior and have them give specific examples of what they have done. It's also helpful to put them in different situations. For instance, if you have a multibranch library, you should give applicants a chance to interact with staff and customers at some or all of the branches.

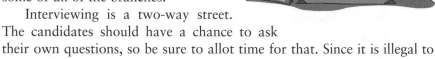

Interviewing is a two-way street. The candidates should have a chance to ask their own questions, so be sure to allot time for that. Since it is illegal to ask candidates certain questions such as their marital status, religion, or age, your first question could be something like, "Please tell us a bit about yourself and why you are interested in this particular job." This open-ended question helps people relax, and you can tell a good deal about people when they talk about themselves.

After each interview, board members should share their impressions with one another while they are still fresh in members' minds. Divergent ratings can be discussed and clarified. It is useful for board members to exchange information so that their perceptions can be brought into alignment, if possible. If it is impossible to determine a favorite, it might be a good idea to pick two or three finalists and invite them back for further interviews. This can even be done by phone. Last but not least, references should be checked.

Step 5
Hire the director

When a hiring decision has been made, the board chair is usually designated to conduct the final negotiations and terms of employment. This should be done quickly to ease the stress of everyone concerned. Unsuccessful candidates should be informed *immediately*. You may have had the unsettling experience of interviewing for a job and then never hearing about it again except through the grapevine. This is very unprofessional. If candidates who did not get the job want to know why they weren't hired, it is common courtesy to give them an honest answer. This will help them when they apply for different positions in the future.

Step 6
Establish mutual expectations

The probationary period for most employees, including the director, is from six to twelve months. When a new director begins his or her relationship with the board of trustees, it is useful to establish your mutual expectations at the outset. Such a discussion offers opportunities to understand what each needs from the others to carry out all the responsibilities. The library director may sign a work agreement or, in some libraries, a formal contract with the board. Check with your state library to see how this process works in your state. It is wise to think of the board and the director as a team working together for the success of the library program. At this point, it is also helpful to go over the bylaws to ensure a mutual understanding of them. Other matters will also need to be covered in a general orientation for the new director, but staff members can do much of that.

Step 7
Celebrate

The best start for a new director is a celebration. You and the other members of your board worked hard, and you hired a person in whom you have confidence. A party is definitely in order so that staff, Friends of the Library, customers, and other stakeholders can meet the new director. It will be a step in the right direction toward a new future.

Disciplinary Action, Including Firing

There is nothing sadder than observing an organization suffering under mediocre management. It just seems to plod along, rarely achieving any progress and barely keeping up with the cost of living. Then there are the organizations that people whisper about because of high staff turnover and unexpected board resignations. Both organizations are in need of new leadership. And you, as a board member, need to *do something about it.* The problem is that the solution is unpleasant. It involves conflict and risk, but if you do it right, you will be serving your community as it deserves to be served.

Probationary evaluations

Probationary periods for employees should be stipulated in your personnel policy. This is a critical time for the board to establish a good working relationship with the director.

It's wise to evaluate the director midway into the probationary period so you can assess his or her progress toward the goals that were set initially. This is also a good time to discuss any board concerns that may have arisen, keeping in mind that it takes time on both sides to adapt to different work styles and personalities. Once again, honesty and candor should be the bywords. If there are improvements to be made on the part of the director, they need to be made before the end of the probation. Clarify what those improvements will be and what resources the director might need to accomplish them. You will still want the person to succeed at this point.

At the end of the probationary period, there should be another evaluation. This is when the board decides whether to keep the director on a permanent basis. If all is not well and the board has made a sincere effort to assist the director, then it is necessary to terminate employment. You must have objective documentation of your reasons for letting the person go, and it must be done before the evaluation meeting. If the library has a human resources department, you should be working closely with it at this point.

The probationary period is a sensitive and crucial time in the relationship between a board and a director. It's tempting to wipe the sweat off your brow and say, "Well, we went through all that hiring business and we finally have a director. Now we can relax and let the person do the work." This is not a smart approach. That first six or twelve months are just as important as the screening process you went through to hire the director. Too many boards fail to be diligent in the probationary period and end up with a much worse problem in the long run. To discover three years down the road that the person is in over his or her head or would be better suited to a different job can mean years of turmoil for the board and the library staff. And it definitely will affect the success of the library's programs. Furthermore, it is far easier (and better for your director) if the decision to terminate is made within the probationary period. If you have duly performed the midpoint and concluding evaluations and have carefully documented your concerns, you will have no legal problem with the termination. And the director will have learned a great deal about him- or herself for any future employment.

Corrective action

Even if the director makes it through the probationary period, problems can still arise. They can be related either to performance or to behavior. The director *must* be evaluated on a regular basis. If the board and the director are doing well together and progress is being made, the sessions will probably be informative and positive, continuing to cement the team relationship. However, if there are problems, corrective action needs to be taken. This is not a disciplinary step but rather an effort to get things back on track.

Corrective action involves a written plan of action, and to succeed it requires participation from both the board and the director. Basically, it is an agreement, similar to a contract, that specifies what needs to be improved, by when, what it will take to improve it, and how improvement will be verified. You and your board colleagues must commit to following through with any actions agreed to on your part. You should also be monitoring progress and deciding what to do if the promised change does not take place.

Terminating the director

If the expectations and terms of the corrective action plan are not met, the board needs to decide whether or not to fire the director. This decision can be made in an executive session, but it must be authorized in a public session. It is wise at this point to hire an attorney if the board does not already have one on retainer. Of course, if the library is a municipal one with a governing board, you will have free access to the city attorney. And if you are on an advisory board, an attorney will be provided.

Check your state law at this point to see if it is legal for you to fire *at will* (for any cause at any time) or *for cause* (as indicated in the law itself). Again, check your personnel policy to see what is spelled out for justifiable terminations. The usual reasons for termination are:

- incompetence
- gross insubordination
- alcoholism or addiction affecting job performance
- sexual harassment
- discrimination
- theft
- extensive absenteeism and resulting lack of performance
- verbal or physical abuse

If the decision has been made to terminate the director's employment, a letter of reprimand is in order. The letter, which is the first step in the termination process, acts as a final warning that failure to improve or discontinue problem behavior will result in loss of the job. It must clearly state that it is a letter of reprimand and detail the problem that mandates the reprimand. It also should account for whatever actions have been taken to help solve the problem (e.g., counseling, training) and describe the expected performance or behavior. It is important to hand-deliver this letter and discuss the contents with the director. Usually the board chair and the vice chair take care of this responsibility. This letter of reprimand becomes a part of the director's personnel file. Once again, if the library has a human resources department, you should be seeking its assistance.

Negotiations

When discussing this matter with your lawyer, consider the following questions:

> Will you allow the director to resign rather than being fired?
>
> Will you agree to provide a reference for the person at least verifying that he or she was indeed the director for a time period?
>
> Will you agree to severance pay?
>
> Will you agree to extending health insurance for a period?
>
> Will you agree to help the person with job searching or rehabilitation?

Loudermill *hearing*

In 1985, the U.S. Supreme Court, upon hearing the case of *Cleveland Board of Education v. Loudermill,* decided that the director is entitled to a final hearing to refute the charges stated in a letter that tells him or her that termination is being considered and on what basis. The director then has an opportunity to review the case and explain in a hearing why the action would be a mistake. The director has the option of requesting a hearing or not, but the "*Loudermill* letter" must be sent.

Letter of termination

Before firing the director publicly, a final letter of discipline has to be sent. This needs to be a formal letter that includes the following:

- restatement of performance or behavioral issues
- statement of negative effects on the library
- specific expectations that have not been met
- description of any counseling or training provided
- a list of corrective action agreements

- statement of board motion to terminate the director's employment
- settlement agreements
- effective date of termination

The letter should be written by a lawyer or human resources manager, but the board will send it to the director in their names. At their next public meeting, the board must resolve the termination action.

Process is important

Termination sounds like a lengthy and loathsome process, but failure to take each step can result in litigation. If the director feels that he or she was unfairly fired and the steps were not followed, the library could be sued for a good deal of money. You can purchase employment practices liability insurance to protect against allegations of discrimination, harassment, and wrongful termination claims, but the best way to protect yourself is to make sure that you have appropriate and well-written personnel policies.

The director will probably resign before being terminated. No one likes the thought of being fired from a job and having that incident on his or her work record. And few people enjoy the pressure to do something they may be unequipped to do. It might be worth it to the library and the board to negotiate an attractive severance package that will accompany a graceful exit. However, that is akin to sweeping the problem under the rug. Another unsuspecting library will come along and trip over it.

Whatever happens, keep in mind that you are taking a course of action for the good of the library, its staff, and the community. In the long run, you and your fellow trustees will be considered to have done your job successfully.

What Have You Learned from This Chapter?

Answer the following questions:

What is your role in hiring a new director?

If you were hiring a new director right now, what attributes would you be looking for?

Can you think of other places to advertise library positions in addition to those listed in this chapter?

How much does a job application tell you?

Does your library have a contract with your director? What does it cover?

How long is the probationary period for employees in your library?

Were midpoint and end-of-probation evaluations held for your director?

Have you ever taken corrective action with your director?

What is a *Loudermill* letter?

NOTE

1. Kurt J. Jenne and Margaret Henderson, "Hiring a Director for a Nonprofit Agency: A Step-by-Step Guide," *Popular Government* 65, no. 4 (2000):25.

9

Budgets, Liability, and Fund-Raising

You and the Library's Budget

Whether you like it or not, you must become as familiar with your library's financial situation as you are with your own. You cannot afford to say blithely, as I have heard from several trustees, "I leave the library's money matters to others. That's just not my interest." If you are determined to be a successful board member, the budget and other financial matters are as much your concern as they are for anyone else on the board. Financial matters can be very confusing, depending upon what state you live in. Alas, no two states appear to be alike when it comes to funding for public libraries! So the first thing you can do is become familiar with how your state operates when it comes to funding its libraries. Table 9.1 will help you determine your principal funding source.

Library districts

While most libraries are city or county libraries whose funding comes from various local tax sources lumped into a "general fund," nineteen states have district legislation for libraries. This means that some libraries or library systems can be considered a taxing district with the authority to levy a tax that is exclusively for libraries. The level of taxing authority is carefully regulated by state law. For instance, in the state of Washington, a library district may not tax more than $.50 per $1,000 worth of property evaluation. But basically, a library with taxing authority is in a better position to have continuity of funding than one that must seek an annual

Type of library	Power base of board	Source of funds	Your level of responsibility
City or municipal	Part of city government	City general fund	Advisory and possibly advocacy
City or municipal	Independent	City general fund	Oversight and advocacy; copresenter at budget meetings
County	Part of county government	County general fund	Advisory and possibly advocacy
County	Independent	Country general fund	Oversight and advocacy; copresenter at budget meetings
Library district	Taxing authority	Direct property tax	Budget refinement, authorizer, taxing level advisor
Federation/ consortium/ regional coordinator	Contract negotiator	From budgets of member libraries	Oversight, advocacy, and negotiation

TABLE 9.1   Where does your library fit?

appropriation. Again, you must consult your state library laws to determine your library's funding situation.

Your role as a governing trustee in a taxing district is just as critical as your role in other library funding situations. The library director, possibly in conjunction with the business manager and other staff, will develop a draft budget. You and the other trustees will study the budget closely to ensure that it conforms to the goals and strategies you developed in the strategic plan, and you may refine it a bit (without micromanaging it). You will then have a role in formally authorizing the budget before it is sent to the city or the county assessor. You will receive tax proceeds either once or twice a year, according to your state law.

Federations, consortia, and regional libraries

Public libraries may be a part of or at the head of a group of libraries that cooperate to provide certain services. Each library will have its own funding authority (city, county, district) but will pay an annual membership fee to a coordinating library to operate the desired services. The purpose of this sort of organization is to be able to offer services for less than it would cost each library to offer them on an individual basis. The economy of scale is at work here, just as it is in other library systems. Again, your own state law will determine what sorts of library organizations are possible within your state.

As a board member of a library that participates in one of these arrangements, you have oversight and advocacy responsibilities toward your own library as well as a role in negotiations with the coordinating library. You need to hold the coordinating library board accountable for seeing that your library receives the services you are paying for.

As a member of the board of the coordinating library, you have oversight over the budget. This includes good faith negotiating with the member libraries. It also entails a degree of political acuity to maintain good relations with the staff and boards of the member libraries whose goodwill determines your existence.

City and county libraries

Public libraries are considered local government services, along with police, fire department, transportation, road repair, water department, and refuse collection. Each of these entities needs to develop an annual budget and present it to the local taxing authority. Public officials are fond of explaining the budget process as the cutting up of a pie. Unfortunately, the library or library system often gets a smaller share of that pie than the other services, particularly the fire and police departments. It's a difficult situation, but there are things you can do to help city council members or county commissioners put the library in the right perspective.

Your role as a trustee is to make sure your budget reflects the goals that you set in your strategic plan. Work closely with your director and library staff to make sure you understand the budget. If you don't, say something. The budget should not be a byzantine document that only an accountant can interpret; it should be clear and self-explanatory. It is helpful to have an accompanying narrative for further clarification.

When presenting the annual budget to the city council or the county commission, an astute board will attend the budget hearing en masse, with library supporters in tow. There is power in numbers! The board chair should make the presentation, with the library director in attendance to answer questions. If at all possible, present the budget with facts and figures that prove that the library is a *public value and improves the quality of life in the community.*

In chapter 4 on advocacy I pointed out that the goals of the library need to adhere to those of the city or county. Illustrate the progress that you are making toward those goals as a part of your budget presentation. If the demographics of the area indicate a problem with literacy or a rising population of a particular minority, show how the library is offering opportunities for lifelong learning or responding to the needs of the minority population. Put yourself in the position of a council member or a commissioner and tell them what you would want to hear in the way you would need to hear (and see) the budget to understand it. It helps if you have kept council members and commissioners informed about what is going on in the library throughout the year. Do not make the budget hearing the only time they get to see the board.

I know of a particular library board and director who have gained a lot of mileage out of having one or two council representatives attend a board meeting to discuss the library's progress and financial needs and to offer their advice. Those folks go back to their respective council seats feeling as if they have a stake in the library's budget. Good politics, folks!

Ongoing budget responsibilities

All board members, whether their role is advisory or governing, need to have regular updates on the progress of the budget from the director throughout the year. In most libraries, there will be a budget status report at every board meeting. Because the tax proceeds come in irregularly, it is important to see that the library has a contingency fund to stay out of the red. Moving funds from one line of the budget to another ought to be done with board approval if it is over a certain amount. That and other money issues should be addressed in the library's financial policy. Unforeseen events—a leaky roof, a natural disaster, or a broken pipe—will invariably occur. Again, contingency funds are a must in a library budget.

Do not be upset if this aspect of library board service is the most difficult learning curve for you. As a tax-supported public entity, you will be under the magnifying glass of the tax-paying public. Consequently, our lawmakers have ensured that there are myriad laws surrounding the spending of those funds.

Liability (or the Cost of Doing Good Things)

Governing boards of public libraries are legally responsible for their decisions. They must conform to state and federal laws as well as their own bylaws. One of the first things you should do when you join a board is have a discussion with your board chair or library director about the issue of liability. Generally speaking, you are not considered to have power as an individual; your power comes from having a seat on the board. Your state statute will have a section that applies to the liability incurred by those who are local governmental entities—and that means you as a board member of a public library.

If you are a member of an advisory board, you do not have to worry about liability unless you do something illegal as an individual. If you are a member of a municipal library, you need to see if you are covered by the city insurance. County library boards may be covered by county insurance, but it is always wise to make sure of that coverage. Don't take it for granted. Because of the very real concerns about liability insurance and legal policy, the common concerns committee of the Association for Library Trustees and Advocates and the Public Library Association adopted the following statement:

> It should be considered mandatory that every library have an adequate level of insurance coverage.
>
> If any claim or action not covered by insurance of State Statute is instigated against a trustee, officer, employee, or volunteer or the Library System arising out of an act or omission by a trustee, officer, employee, or volunteer acting in good faith for a purpose considered to be in the best interest of the System; or if any claim or action not covered by insurance of State Statute is instituted against a trustee, officer, employee, or volunteer allegedly arising out of an act or omission occurring within the scope of his/her duties as such a trustee, officer, employee, or volunteer; the System should at the request of the trustee, officer, employee, or volunteer:
>
> • Appear and defend against the claim or action; and

- Pay or indemnify the trustee, officer, employee, or volunteer for a judgment and court costs, based on such claim or action; and

- Pay or indemnify the trustee, officer, employee, or volunteer for a compromise or settlement of such claim or action, providing the settlement is approved by the Board of Trustees.

To ensure that you are adequately protected against lawsuits, check to see whether the library has errors and omissions insurance. Errors and omissions insurance should cover any area where a board might incur liability. That includes:

- acts in excess of authority

- errors in acts

- negligence

- nonfeasance or failure to act

- intentional violations of civil law

- acts in violation of the law

Broken windows, faulty water heaters, and leaking toilets all happen as a matter of course in a library. And there will always be the person who slips on the sidewalk, the customer who gets hit in the head by a book, or the man who complains about a flat tire caused by thumbtacks in the parking lot. An annual risk assessment of the library's physical facilities is a wise precaution to take, and a good property insurance policy is a necessary investment.

The best advice for a board member is to *pay attention*. Probably the greatest liability risk for a library board is nonfeasance—failure to act, failure to do the job as it ought to be done.

So what can you do as an individual? Read those board packets that come every month prior to your meetings. Pay attention to the budget reports and the annual audit. Really know, understand, and follow the library's policies. Don't vote on an issue unless you thoroughly understand the options and feel comfortable with your decision. Don't hesitate to seek legal counsel when needed. Be familiar with your state's Open Public Meetings Act, federal copyright compliance laws, your library's compliance with the Americans with Disabilities Act, and public records availability. It is not necessary to be paranoid about these things, but it is necessary to be knowledgeable. We live in litigious times, and it helps to be prepared.

Fund-Raising

Libraries are expensive operations, and if a library is successful, the facilities wear out every twenty years or so—some even sooner. Buildings and furnishings are expensive; technology is expensive; quality employees should be expensive; and keeping the collection current with information and popular materials is expensive. Few public libraries get enough money from their funding authorities to cover all these expenses. The balance has to be met through fund-raising activities.

Friends of the Library

For years, most libraries have enjoyed the support of customers and supporters who form groups called the Friends of the Library. Their purpose is to raise money for the library and to advocate for it with local, state, and federal officials. In some libraries, the Friends groups are large, vocal, and very active; in others, they struggle to survive. Much depends upon leadership and support from the board of trustees and the library staff.

Some Friends groups raise money by holding bake sales, book sales (often library castoffs), plant sales, and other low-key affairs. Other Friends groups operate library gift shops—much like museum gift shops—that appeal to tasteful shoppers looking for unique items. Some Friends groups hold art shows, antique shows, and silent auctions. These ventures can raise significant funds for the library.

Friends groups are usually 501(c)3 organizations (nonprofit, tax-exempt) with officers and bylaws. They raise funds and decide how they are to be spent. This can cause friction with the board and staff if the priorities of the Friends group do not match those in the strategic plan. To avoid that possibility, try to involve the Friends in planning for the library. Designate a member of the board to act as a liaison to the group and attend their meetings.

Foundations

Another funding source gaining popularity is the library foundation. Private foundations are structures through which people can give to a good cause, and what better cause than the local library? The gift dollars are tax exempt and are certainly needed by the library. As a separate legal entity, much like a Friends group, the foundation is nonprofit and formed for the purpose of supporting and fund-raising for the library. The advantage of having a foundation is that it can do things that the library, as a government entity, cannot, such as:

- apply for grants for which public libraries do not qualify
- accept stocks, property, and cash
- provide a planned giving opportunity
- act as the depositor for either an endowment or a memorial fund
- invest the funds in ways that are more flexible than those allowed to public agencies

Establishing a library foundation is much like establishing a library Friends group. A board of directors has to be formed and the basic legal steps need to be taken. The articles of incorporation and bylaws need to be prepared and approved, and the application for a 501(c)3 status must be made to the IRS. Since public funds cannot be used to establish a private foundation, private funds will be needed for legal fees and document filing fees. The ideal situation would be to have both a Friends group and a library foundation.

Grants

There are two kinds of grants—those coming from public entities and those coming from private organizations. Public libraries are eligible for only a few, but their foundations may be eligible for more. The public grant funding most familiar to public libraries comes from the federal government and is initially allocated to state libraries. It was enacted in 1956 as the Library Services and Construction Act (LSCA). It established library systems in many states, provided funds for many library buildings, and paid for many cornerstone statewide library projects. Direct grants were provided to many libraries as well.

In 1996, Congress replaced LSCA with the Library Services and Technology Act (LSTA) and changed its funding emphasis from establishing systems and erecting buildings to providing information through state, regional, and international electronic networks. Each state library, with the assistance of an advisory council, establishes its own priorities for the grant funds. It is still possible to obtain grant funds from LSTA, but you must be familiar with your own state's program.

There are several other sources of private grants. Locally, you might check with your PTA, the League of Women Voters, the American Association of University Women, Rotary, and other service clubs. Nationally, depending upon what you are trying to do, there are sources for funding literacy, history, early childhood development, diversity, and other such focused programs. The Internet is a marvelous source of information on grants for libraries. Several websites are listed in appendix B of this book.

The Last Word about Funding

Funding for libraries has always been difficult to obtain, but one of your main responsibilities as a trustee is to make sure that your library is as well funded as it can be. One way you can help is to clarify for your constituents how the library is funded. You would be surprised at how many people have no idea that the taxes they pay support libraries. Most Americans seem to feel that the library is one of life's basics, like clean air, and that libraries don't need very much to survive. Of course, both assumptions are false. Make a point of educating the citizens of your community about the realities of library funding.

The following quote is instructive: "An increasingly skeptical public withholds its support when it is not convinced that an organization has made a serious commitment to quality and excellence. Before organizations mount fund-raising drives, they should ask themselves what they have to offer and whether they are presenting it in a convincing manner."[1]

So don't be afraid to ask for money for the library. But ask for it in a proactive, positive, well-informed manner that will convince people that the library is worthy of their full support.

What Have You Learned from This Chapter?

Answer the following questions:

Where does the funding for your library come from?

Do you feel positive that your board is doing all it can do to fund your library adequately?

How would you describe your relationship with your funding authority? What can you do to improve it?

If the library has a Friend's group, how would you describe its usefulness? What can you do to improve it?

How familiar are you with your state's LSTA program? How is the money being used currently?

If you were going to talk to a potential donor to your library foundation, what would you say to convince him or her that the library is deserving of a gift of funds?

NOTE

1. Edgar Stoesz and Chester Raber, *Doing Good Better: How to Be an Effective Board Member of a Nonprofit Organization* (Intercourse, Pa.: Good Books, 1994), 62.

10

You Are Not Alone

While working as a consultant for the Washington State Library, I instituted a state trustee conference that would occur every two years. The conference, patterned on a template developed by the Association for Library Trustees and Advocates (ALTA), is called the Workshop in Library Leadership and is still happening thanks to the state library consultants. About 120 trustees from around the state come together biannually to attend workshops over a two-day period. At one such conference, a woman came up to thank me, saying, "I now know that I am not alone. I can't tell you how good this feels!"

Let me assure you that you are not alone either. If you and your fellow board members need assistance, advice, or just a shoulder to cry on, there are people and resources to help you. In this chapter, I will try to identify the major sources of help.

State Libraries

Every state has an office that accepts federal funding on behalf of the state's libraries. For the most part, these are known as state libraries. Although some have little more than an office that is part of another state agency, most states still have state libraries and state librarians. Some are actual libraries that support the information needs of state government. Some state libraries focus on the state's history, and some contain and coordinate the state's archival collection. All of them provide development and consultation services to all the libraries in the state.

State library development departments can be counted on for advice, interpretation of state law, information about federal grants, guidance on various state projects for libraries, and other kinds of aid, such as training.

Check to see what services your state library provides for trustees. Each one has a website listing services, contact names, e-mail addresses, and phone numbers. If training is provided, the classes will be listed. The site might even offer online registration. One of the really wonderful things about attending a statewide workshop for trustees is that you will meet other trustees who may have many things in common with you and your board. Perhaps they will have already found a solution to a problem with which you are struggling or vice versa.

State Associations

Every state also has a state library association. In some cases, trustees will find that there is a section of the organization just for them. In other cases, there will be a separate state association for library trustees. These associations usually meet in conference once a year, have a website, and are eager for new members. What a wonderful way to meet people in other towns, counties, and systems who have the same job you do! The state trustee organizations usually offer workshops, newsletters, and websites, as well as awards for excellence among boards and individual trustees. Don't shut yourself off from these opportunities for learning and networking.

Association for Library Trustees and Advocates

I have already mentioned ALTA, the esteemed national association for library trustees. The ALTA mission statement reads as follows:

> The Association for Library Trustees and Advocates promotes and ensures outstanding library service through educational programs that develop excellence in trusteeship and actions that advocate access to information for all.

There are two opportunities a year to attend ALA conferences and participate with the other members of ALTA. The educational programs are provided by the best in the library world; the networking is very helpful; and the e-mail discussion group can be there for you at any time. ALTA is the perfect source for information about advocacy, providing lists of resources and materials. Its website is a composite of great information with helpful links to all the online resources you might need.

Private Consultants

There are times when a private consultant—an outside objective person with training and credentials—can be very helpful. Sometimes a state library consultant doesn't have time to spend on a problem that may take months to resolve. Sometimes you need an outside facilitator to deal with a sticky situation in which you would like to keep a low profile. Perhaps you need expertise that is not available from your state library, or maybe you have a job that you don't want staff involved with: there are many reasons why a private consultant can be the exact type of help you need.

Consultants can not only provide sound advice but they can also facilitate difficult meetings or strategic planning processes, arrange and facilitate focus groups, provide documentation from the focus groups, or even conduct workshops. These consultants are not cheap, but they are probably worth every penny they charge. The typical fee for library consultants these days is around $125 to $150 per hour plus travel expenses.

Your state library and your state association probably maintain a list of consultants and their specialty areas. There are sources on the Internet that are easily located, and ALA publishes a list of consultants on a regular basis.

Other Sources

As a library trustee, you operate very much like the board members of other public, nonprofit organizations. There are countless excellent publications available—even from your own library—on the subject of board service in general and libraries in particular. I have cited both print and online materials in the writing of this book. Finding the information I needed was incredibly easy with the Google search engine. I have included a brief list of online information resources in the back of this book, keeping in mind that websites come and go with the wind. If you are not partial to the Internet, there are books and magazine articles aplenty just waiting for you.

Last Words

There is no quiz for you this time. I just want to wish you good luck. I am confident that you will join the ranks of successful library trustees. You may not make it into *Who's Who,* but we librarians know that millions of people in the United States have great library service thanks to your efforts.

Appendix

Resolution on the U.S.A. Patriot Act and Related Measures That Infringe on the Rights of Library Users

WHEREAS, The American Library Association affirms the responsibility of the leaders of the United States to protect and preserve the freedoms that are the foundation of our democracy; and

WHEREAS, Libraries are a critical force for promoting the free flow and unimpeded distribution of knowledge and information for individuals, institutions, and communities; and

WHEREAS, The American Library Association holds that suppression of ideas undermines a democratic society; and

WHEREAS, Privacy is essential to the exercise of free speech, free thought, and free association; and, in a library, the subject of users' interests should not be examined or scrutinized by others; and

WHEREAS, Certain provisions of the USA PATRIOT Act, the revised Attorney General Guidelines to the Federal Bureau of Investigation, and other related measures expand the authority of the federal government to investigate citizens and non-citizens, to engage in surveillance, and to threaten civil rights and liberties guaranteed under the United States Constitution and Bill of Rights; and

WHEREAS, The USA PATRIOT Act and other recently enacted laws, regulations, and guidelines increase the likelihood that the activities of library users, including their use of computers to browse the Web or access e-mail, may be under government surveillance without their knowledge or consent; now, therefore, be it

RESOLVED, That the American Library Association opposes any use of governmental power to suppress the free and open exchange of knowledge and information or to intimidate individuals exercising free inquiry; and, be it further

RESOLVED, That the American Library Association encourages all librarians, library administrators, library governing bodies, and library advocates to educate their users, staff, and communities about the process for compliance with the USA PATRIOT Act and other related measures and about the dangers to individual privacy and the confidentiality of library records resulting from those measures; and, be it further

RESOLVED, That the American Library Association urges librarians everywhere to defend and support user privacy and free and open access to knowledge and information; and, be it further

RESOLVED, That the American Library Association will work with other organizations, as appropriate, to protect the rights of inquiry and free expression; and, be it further

RESOLVED, That the American Library Association will take actions as appropriate to obtain and publicize information about the surveillance of libraries and library users by law enforcement agencies and to assess the impact on library users and their communities; and, be it further

RESOLVED, That the American Library Association urges all libraries to adopt and implement patron privacy and record retention policies that affirm that "the collection of personally identifiable information should only be a matter of routine or policy when necessary for the fulfillment of the mission of the library" (*ALA Privacy: An Interpretation of the Library Bill of Rights*); and, be it further

RESOLVED, That the American Library Association considers sections of the USA PATRIOT Act are a present danger to the constitutional rights and privacy rights of library users and urges the United States Congress to:

1. Provide active oversight of the implementation of the USA PATRIOT Act and other related measures, and the revised Attorney General Guidelines to the Federal Bureau of Investigation;
2. Hold hearings to determine the extent of the surveillance on library users and their communities; and

3. Amend or change the sections of these laws and the guidelines that threaten or abridge the rights of inquiry and free expression; and, be it further

RESOLVED, That this resolution be forwarded to the President of the United States, to the Attorney General of the United States, to Members of both Houses of Congress, to the library community, and to others as appropriate.

Initiated by: Committee on Legislation

Cosponsored by: Committee on Legislation and Intellectual Freedom Committee

Endorsed by: OITP Advisory Committee, LITA

Endorsed in principle by: ACRL, ALTA Executive Board, ALSC, ASCLA, AASL Legislation Committee

Prior History: CD#19.1 January 2002, CD#20.5 January 2002, CD#20.3 January 2002

On Wednesday, January 29, 2003, Council adopted 20.1 as amended.

Useful Websites
for Library Trustees

American Library Association: www.ala.org

Association for Library Trustees and Advocates: www.ala.org/alta

BoardSource: www.boardsource.org

CompassPoint. *Board Café* newsletter: http://compasspoint.org

Copyright Clearance Center: www.copyright.com

Foundation Center: www.fdncenter.org

Friends of Libraries U.S.A.: www.folusa.com

The Grantsmanship Center: www.tgci.com

Library of Congress. U.S. Copyright Office: www.copyright.gov

United Way of America. Outcome Measurement Resource Network: http://national.unitedway.org/outcomes

Workforce Management: www.workforce.com

Your Own Useful Websites

State library association _____

State library _____

Your library _____

Your city _____

Your county _____

Your online library directory _____

Appendix

C

Freedom to Read Statement

The freedom to read is essential to our democracy. It is continuously under attack. Private groups and public authorities in various parts of the country are working to remove or limit access to reading materials, to censor content in schools, to label "controversial" views, to distribute lists of "objectionable" books or authors, and to purge libraries. These actions apparently rise from a view that our national tradition of free expression is no longer valid; that censorship and suppression are needed to avoid the subversion of politics and the corruption of morals. We, as citizens devoted to reading and as librarians and publishers responsible for disseminating ideas, wish to assert the public interest in the preservation of the freedom to read.

Most attempts at suppression rest on a denial of the fundamental premise of democracy: that the ordinary citizen, by exercising critical judgment, will accept the good and reject the bad. The censors, public and private, assume that they should determine what is good and what is bad for their fellow citizens.

We trust Americans to recognize propaganda and misinformation, and to make their own decisions about what they read and believe. We do not believe they need the help of censors to assist them in this task. We do not believe they are prepared to sacrifice their heritage of a free press in order to be "protected" against what others think may be bad for them. We believe they still favor free enterprise in ideas and expression.

These efforts at suppression are related to a larger pattern of pressures being brought against education, the press, art and images, films, broadcast media, and the Internet. The problem is not only one of actual censorship. The shadow of fear cast by these pressures leads, we suspect, to an even larger voluntary curtailment of expression by those who seek to avoid controversy.

Such pressure toward conformity is perhaps natural to a time of accelerated change. And yet suppression is never more dangerous than in such a time of social tension. Freedom has given the United States the elasticity to endure strain. Freedom keeps open the path of novel and creative solutions, and enables change to come by choice. Every silencing of a heresy, every enforcement of an orthodoxy, diminishes the toughness and resilience of our society and leaves it the less able to deal with controversy and difference.

Now as always in our history, reading is among our greatest freedoms. The freedom to read and write is almost the only means for making generally available ideas or manners of expression that can initially command only a small audience. The written word is the natural medium for the new idea and the untried voice from which come the original contributions to social growth. It is essential to the extended discussion that serious thought requires, and to the accumulation of knowledge and ideas into organized collections.

We believe that free communication is essential to the preservation of a free society and a creative culture. We believe that these pressures toward conformity present the danger of limiting the range and variety of inquiry and expression on which our democracy and our culture depend. We believe that every American community must jealously guard the freedom to publish and to circulate, in order to preserve its own freedom to read. We believe that publishers and librarians have a profound responsibility to give validity to that freedom to read by making it possible for the readers to choose freely from a variety of offerings. The freedom to read is guaranteed by the Constitution. Those with faith in free people will stand firm on these constitutional guarantees of essential rights and will exercise the responsibilities that accompany these rights.

We therefore affirm these propositions:

1. *It is in the public interest for publishers and librarians to make available the widest diversity of views and expressions, including those that are unorthodox or unpopular with the majority.*

Creative thought is by definition new, and what is new is different. The bearer of every new thought is a rebel until that idea is refined and tested. Totalitarian systems attempt to maintain themselves in power by the ruthless suppression of any concept that challenges the established orthodoxy. The power of a democratic system to adapt to change is vastly strengthened by the freedom of its citizens to choose widely from among conflicting opinions offered freely to them. To stifle every nonconformist idea at birth would mark the end of the democratic process. Furthermore, only through the constant activity of weighing and selecting can the democratic mind attain the strength demanded by times like these. We need to know not only what we believe but why we believe it.

> 2. *Publishers, librarians, and booksellers do not need to endorse every idea or presentation they make available. It would conflict with the public interest for them to establish their own political, moral, or aesthetic views as a standard for determining what should be published or circulated.*

Publishers and librarians serve the educational process by helping to make available knowledge and ideas required for the growth of the mind and the increase of learning. They do not foster education by imposing as mentors the patterns of their own thought. The people should have the freedom to read and consider a broader range of ideas than those that may be held by any single librarian or publisher or government or church. It is wrong that what one can read should be confined to what another thinks proper.

> 3. *It is contrary to the public interest for publishers or librarians to bar access to writings on the basis of the personal history or political affiliations of the author.*

No art or literature can flourish if it is to be measured by the political views or private lives of its creators. No society of free people can flourish that draws up lists of writers to whom it will not listen, whatever they may have to say.

> 4. *There is no place in our society for efforts to coerce the taste of others, to confine adults to the reading matter deemed suitable for adolescents, or to inhibit the efforts of writers to achieve artistic expression.*

To some, much of modern expression is shocking. But is not much of life itself shocking? We cut off literature at the source if we prevent writers from dealing with the stuff of life. Parents and teachers have a responsibility to prepare the young to meet the diversity of experiences in life to which they will be exposed, as they have a responsibility to help them learn to think critically for themselves. These are affirmative responsibilities, not to be discharged simply by preventing them from reading works for which they are not yet prepared. In these matters values differ, and values cannot be legislated; nor can machinery be devised that will suit the demands of one group without limiting the freedom of others.

5. *It is not in the public interest to force a reader to accept with any expression the prejudgment of a label characterizing it or its author as subversive or dangerous.*

The ideal of labeling presupposes the existence of individuals or groups with wisdom to determine by authority what is good or bad for the citizen. It presupposes that individuals must be directed in making up their minds about the ideas they examine. But Americans do not need others to do their thinking for them.

6. *It is the responsibility of publishers and librarians, as guardians of the people's freedom to read, to contest encroachments upon that freedom by individuals or groups seeking to impose their own standards or tastes upon the community at large.*

It is inevitable in the give and take of the democratic process that the political, the moral, or the aesthetic concepts of an individual or group will occasionally collide with those of another individual or group. In a free society individuals are free to determine for themselves what they wish to read, and each group is free to determine what it will recommend to its freely associated members. But no group has the right to take the law into its own hands, and to impose its own concept of politics or morality upon other members of a democratic society. Freedom is no freedom if it is accorded only to the accepted and the inoffensive.

7. *It is the responsibility of publishers and librarians to give full meaning to the freedom to read by providing books that enrich the quality and diversity of thought and expression. By the exercise of this*

affirmative responsibility, they can demonstrate that the answer to a "bad" book is a good one, the answer to a "bad" idea is a good one.

The freedom to read is of little consequence when the reader cannot obtain matter fit for that reader's purpose. What is needed is not only the absence of restraint, but the positive provision of opportunity for the people to read the best that has been thought and said. Books are the major channel by which the intellectual inheritance is handed down, and the principal means of its testing and growth. The defense of the freedom to read requires of all publishers and librarians the utmost of their faculties, and deserves of all citizens the fullest of their support.

We state these propositions neither lightly nor as easy generalizations. We here stake out a lofty claim for the value of the written word. We do so because we believe that it is possessed of enormous variety and usefulness, worthy of cherishing and keeping free. We realize that the application of these propositions may mean the dissemination of ideas and manners of expression that are repugnant to many persons. We do not state these propositions in the comfortable belief that what people read is unimportant. We believe rather that what people read is deeply important; that ideas can be dangerous; but that the suppression of ideas is fatal to a democratic society. Freedom itself is a dangerous way of life, but it is ours.

This statement was originally issued in May of 1953 by the Westchester Conference of the American Library Association and the American Book Publishers Council, which in 1970 consolidated with the American Educational Publishers Institute to become the Association of American Publishers.

Adopted June 25, 1953; revised January 28, 1972, January 16, 1991, July 12, 2000, by the ALA Council and the AAP Freedom to Read Committee.

A Joint Statement by:

    American Library Association

    Association of American Publishers

Subsequently Endorsed by:

    American Association of University Professors

    American Booksellers Foundation for Free Expression

    American Society of Journalists and Authors

The American Society of Newspaper Editors

Anti-Defamation League of B'nai B'rith

Association of American University Presses

Center for Democracy & Technology

The Children's Book Council

The Electronic Frontier Foundation

Feminists for Free Expression

Freedom to Read Foundation

International Reading Association

The Media Institute

National Coalition Against Censorship

National PTA

Parents, Families and Friends of Lesbians and Gays

People for the American Way

Pen American Center

Student Press Law Center

The Thomas Jefferson Center for the Protection of Free Expression

Library Bill of Rights

The American Library Association affirms that all libraries are forums for information and ideas, and that the following basic policies should guide their services.

    I. Books and other library resources should be provided for the interest, information, and enlightenment of all people of the community the library serves. Materials should not be excluded because of the origin, background, or views of those contributing to their creation.

    II. Libraries should provide materials and information presenting all points of view on current and historical issues. Materials should not be proscribed or removed because of partisan or doctrinal disapproval.

    III. Libraries should challenge censorship in the fulfillment of their responsibility to provide information and enlightenment.

    IV. Libraries should cooperate with all persons and groups concerned with resisting abridgment of free expression and free access to ideas.

    V. A person's right to use a library should not be denied or abridged because of origin, age, background, or views.

    VI. Libraries which make exhibit spaces and meeting rooms available to the public they serve should make such facilities available on an equitable basis, regardless of the beliefs or affiliations of individuals or groups requesting their use.

Adopted June 18, 1948.
Amended February 2, 1961, and January 23, 1980,
inclusion of "age" reaffirmed January 23, 1996,
by the ALA Council.

INDEX

Mary Y. Moore is an independent library consultant, trainer, and facilitator who lives in Olympia, Washington. She has been a professional librarian in special, academic, and public libraries for almost forty years. Before joining the staff of the Washington State Library as head of library development in 1983, Moore ran a five-county rural public library system in Montana.

She has worked with library boards for many years both as a public library director and consultant. She has also been a member of several boards, serving in the capacity of both member and chair.

Moore earned her master's degree at Drexel University School of Library and Information Science.